William Henry Wheeler

History of the Fens of South Lincolnshire

Being a description of the rivers Witham and Welland and their estuary; and an account of the reclamation and drainage of the fens adjacent thereto.

William Henry Wheeler

History of the Fens of South Lincolnshire
Being a description of the rivers Witham and Welland and their estuary; and an account of the reclamation and drainage of the fens adjacent thereto.

ISBN/EAN: 9783337377403

Printed in Europe, USA, Canada, Australia, Japan

Cover: Foto ©ninafisch / pixelio.de

More available books at **www.hansebooks.com**

HISTORY OF THE FENS

OF

SOUTH LINCOLNSHIRE,

BEING A DESCRIPTION OF THE

RIVERS WITHAM AND WELLAND AND THEIR ESTUARY; AND AN ACCOUNT OF THE RECLAMATION AND DRAINAGE OF THE FENS ADJACENT THERETO.

BY

W. H. WHEELER,
CIVIL ENGINEER.

BOSTON:
J. M. NEWCOMB, PRINTER AND BOOKSELLER,
MARKET PLACE.
LONDON:
SIMPKIN, MARSHALL, AND CO.,
1868.

CONTENTS.

CHAPTER I.
INTRODUCTION AND EARLY HISTORY OF THE FENS.

CHAPTER II.
THE RIVER WITHAM AND THE FENS ADJACENT THERETO.

CHAPTER III.
THE EAST, WEST, AND WILDMORE FENS.

CHAPTER IV.
HOLLAND FEN AND THE BLACK SLUICE DISTRICT.

CHAPTER V.
THE RIVER WELLAND, CROWLAND, AND DEEPING FEN.

CHAPTER VI.
THE ORIGIN AND CONSTITUTION OF THE COURT OF SEWERS.

CHAPTER VII.
BOSTON HARBOUR AND HAVEN.

CHAPTER VIII.
THE ESTUARY, WITH AN ACCOUNT OF THE VARIOUS SCHEMES WHICH HAVE BEEN BROUGHT FORWARD FOR THE IMPROVEMENT OF THE OUTFALL IN CONNECTION WITH THE DRAINAGE AND NAVIGATION.

PLAN OF THE FENS AND THE ESTUARY.

PREFACE.

The author having lately had occasion to examine the documents relating to the Outfall of the Drainage of the Fens, was induced by the interest of the subject to extend his researches into the various works which bear upon their general history and reclamation, and collected together a number of facts and statistics sufficient to enable him to complete a short history of the Fens of this part of the County of Lincoln, which appeared in a series of papers contributed to the Stamford Mercury during the Autumn of last year. He considers that an account of the means which have been adopted for the drainage and enclosure of 250,000 acres of land, a space larger than some of the English counties, which from having been little better than a mere morass, has become one of the richest tracts of agricultural land in the country, must of itself be interesting, however badly the subject may be treated by the author. These papers pretend to no originality or literary merit whatever, but are simply a collection of facts compiled from various works that in any way treat of the subject, many of which are out of print; and the reports of engineers, and other official documents, not accessible to the general public. No complete account of the later history of these Fens exists. The earlier history has been partially described by Sir W. Dugdale, in his treatise on Embanking and Draining, and much interesting matter, bearing on the subject, is to be found in Elstob's History of the Bedford Level, and Ingulph's History of Crowland. Mr. Thompson has also devoted a short space to the Fens; but the design of his work, being confined to a History of the Town of Boston, embraces only a brief outline of the Fen history. From these and various other sources the author has collected his information, and whenever practicable has preferred to use the language of the author he has quoted to that of his own. The History is intended to commence with a full account of the last successful attempt to reclaim the Fens, but in order to render the subject more clear the first chapter will be devoted to a sketch of the original formation of the district and the various changes it has undergone; the second chapter will be devoted to the River Witham and the Fens adjacent thereto; the third to the East, West, and Wildmore Fens; the fourth to the Holland Fen and the Black Sluice district; the fifth to the Welland and Deeping Fen; the sixth contains an account of the origin and constitution of the Court of Sewers; the seventh relates to Boston Harbour and Haven; and the last to the Estuary, and the various schemes which have been brought forward for its improvement in connection with the drainage and navigation.

The accompanying Plan, reduced from the Ordnance Map, has been corrected and adapted by the author specially for this book.

Boston, February, 1868.

CHAPTER I.

INTRODUCTION AND EARLY HISTORY OF THE FENS.

The Great Level of the Fens comprises all that vast tract of land on the east coast, extending southwards, from the high lands in Lincolnshire, for a distance of about 60 miles, and occupying portions of six counties. It is only the history of the northern portion that will be sketched out in these papers, or that part bounded on the north by the Steeping river and the villages of Toynton, Revesby, and the city of Lincoln; on the west by the Car Dyke; and on the south by the river Welland; and comprising the East, West, and Wildmore Fens, the lands adjacent to the Witham, known as the six districts, Holland Fen and the Black Sluice Level, and Deeping Fen and the lands on the north of the Welland.

The Fens have obtained a world-wide notoriety, and a general though very erroneous impression prevails, among those who have not visited this county, that Lincolnshire is a dull and dreary land, to be avoided by all whom necessity or the calls of business do not compel to visit its unattractive scenery. But although the fens include an area of about 500,000 acres (equal in extent to some of the English counties), there yet remains of Lincolnshire about one and a quarter millions of acres, which can vie with any other part of England for the picturesqueness of its scenery and the salubrity of the climate; while the rich grazing and corn lands of the fens stand unrivalled for their productiveness, and are cultivated by inhabitants whose condition, general physique, and health will bear very favourable comparison with any other district of Great Britain.

The original formation of the soil of these fens, although recent in the geological classification, takes us back to a time anterior to the existence of man, when the whole of this district was beneath the waters of the sea. For a depth of nearly 600 feet nothing has been discovered but an aqueous deposit of clay mixed with shells and stones. At the time when this history commences, this deposit had accumulated to such a height as to be above the ordinary tides, and only the lower portion of the Fens, or the parts nearest to the sea, were under ordinary circumstances overflowed by their action. Possibly trees had already grown to a considerable size on the higher portion, or that furthest removed from the sea; and on spots here and there in the lower parts, which had risen higher than the rest—as we see in the villages of Stickney and Sibsey at the present day;—and these were doubtless inhabited by the aborigines of the island. The rest was covered with coarse grass, sometimes available for pasturage, and at others inundated in turns by the overflowings of the rivers and the tides. The land at this time was peopled by the Britons, a rude, uncultivated race of men. Their religion was one that sought the solitudes of woods and dark groves for the observance of their mysterious and sometimes sanguinary rites, and probably the priests availed themselves of the secret recesses of the Fens for the erection of their altars.

In the year 55 B.C. the Roman Generals, ever seeking fresh conquests to add laurels to their arms, first sought out and invaded the island of Britain, and having once obtained a footing found the country so profitable that they remained here for a period of nearly 500 years. While we look to the sober pages of historical facts for a correct knowledge of the doings of bygone days, it is pleasing to allow our imagination to be assisted in realising the events those facts disclose by a perusal of the works of writers of fiction, who have endeavoured to render our ancient history a true and living picture. All who take a delight in this class of literature will call to mind the charming and vivid description of Esca, the British chieftain, a slave at Rome, and the old Roman general, who was reminded by the presence of his Saxon attendant of his buried loves and hopes in the far off woods of conquered Britain, where all his glorious deeds of arms were saddened by the recollection of the fair haired maiden he had seen and wooed in the British forest.

The Romans having once firmly established themselves in the island, maintained their conquest by the presence of a large force, which was stationed at several military depôts, scattered throughout the country. Of these Lincoln became the head quarters of the midland district, or that part of the country then inhabited by the Coritani. The thorough knowledge and appreciation of agricultural arts, ever so prominent in the Romans, would lead them at once to see the value of the large tract of fen land lying so near their station; and the experience they had acquired in enclosing and draining, about this time, similar tracts of marsh land in the south of Italy, and also in the Belgian Provinces, and in constructing through the Pomptine fens a large cut, which served the double purpose of a sewer and a canal, would at once suggest to them the feasibility of reclaiming the great level of the fens. The labour necessary in carrying out the work would provide ample employment for their soldiers and captives; it being ever a practice with the Roman generals to keep the legions from idleness and discontent by constant employment;* and by

---

* Probus prevented the irregularities of the soldiers by employing the legions in constant and useful labours When he commanded in Egypt, Probus executed many considerable works for the splendour of that rich country. The navigation of the Nile was improved, and temples, bridges, porticoes, and palaces were constructed by the hands of the soldiers, who acted by turns as architects, as engineers, and as husbandmen. It was reported of Hannibal that, in order to preserve his troops from the dangerous temptations of idleness, he had obliged them to form large plantations of olive trees along the Coast of Africa . . . . He thus converted into tillage a large and unhealthy tract of marsh ground near Sirmium. . . . . In one of the hottest days of summer, as he severely urged the unwholesome labour of draining the marshes of Sirmium, the soldiers, impatient of fatigue, on a sudden threw down their tools, grasped their swords, and broke out in a furious mutiny, and finally murdered the unfortunate Emperor. Gibbon, cap. XII

this salutary rule they had ever at their disposal a mighty force which enabled them to carry out those vast engineering works, the traces of which, even at the present day, are to be found in every country which they subdued.

Another powerful motive that would lead to the embanking of the fens doubtless arose from the security they afforded to the natives, who, as related by Marcellinus, " not dwelling in the towns but in cottages within fenny places, compassed with thick woods, having hidden whatsoever they had most estimation of, did more annoyance to the wearied Romans than they received from them." In fact the fens formed a sort of camp of refuge for the Britons, as later they did to the Saxons, where it would be impossible for any military force to follow and dislodge them; and it is evident the Romans could neither pasture their cattle on the marshes nor enjoy any security for their property until the natives were hunted out of their retreats.

Having once undertaken the reclamation of the watery waste, the Romans proceeded in the most skilful and artistic manner, pursuing a course that has been taken as a model by the engineers of modern times, being adopted by Mr. Rennie in his scheme for the drainage of the East and West Fens. The work divided itself into two parts—the embanking, to shut out the sea water; and the draining, to void the rainfall falling on the surface of the enclosed land, and also poured on to it from the higher ground adjacent. To effect this latter object a large catchwater drain was made, skirting the borders of the fens, intercepting the water from the high lands, and preventing it pouring on to and inundating the fen. This cut commenced near Lincoln, communicating with the Witham, and extended along the whole western side of the fens till it joined the Welland, and thence continued to the Nene. It was made navigable, and afforded communication between Peterboro' and Lincoln, and also with ships coming by sea, by means of the rivers Nene or Witham, and gave an easy means of transporting military stores and provisions to their inland depôts. The canal is known by the name of the Car Dyke, and its course may be clearly traced at the present day. Ample testimony to the wisdom that designed it is provided by the various projects that have been brought forward by modern engineers for utilising such parts of it as passed through the fens then immediately under their consideration. The course of another artificial cut or drain may be traced in the "Westlode," which drained the low lands towards Crowland and Deeping Fen and emptied into the Welland.

The drainage of the interior of the fens was provided by other cuts, the remains of which are scarcely to be traced now, but there is no doubt the Old Hammond Beck was one of these. These interior drains, which discharged their contents into the rivers, were protected by sluices, but the rivers themselves were embanked and the tides allowed to have their free course, ships navigating the Witham as far as Lincoln.

The sea was shut out from overflowing the low lands by those stupendous embankments which surround the level, and on the integrity of which, at this very time, depends the safety of all this district. One breach in these banks, and in a few hours property to an enormous amount would immediately be destroyed, and the land rendered a scene of desolation. These embankments, as viewed at the present day, give but little idea of the magnitude of the labour involved in their construction. To form a more correct estimate, it must be borne in mind that since that time the land has been raised several feet in height, and the base of them, which at the period of their erection stood above the surrounding ground, now forms part of it. The banks enclosing the portion of the great level to which this history is confined extend to a length of upwards of 50 miles—at so great an expenditure of time and labour was this land reclaimed from the sea.

The great care of the Romans, after having thoroughly embanked and drained the land, was to provide the means of easy communication by the construction of roads. These were not formed on the principle followed by the reclaimers of the fens of our generation, who deemed it sufficient to leave a wide space and call it a road, but were constructed in the most solid and substantial manner, with brick and stones cemented together, and laid in regular courses, with a concrete foundation, and so solidly and firmly were they built that traces are constantly being discovered in a complete state of preservation. The chief road passing through this district was a loop line of the Great North-road, or Ermin-street, which after crossing the river Nene, pursued a N.E. course through Thurlby, Bourn, towards Sleaford, and thence through Ruskington, Dorrington, Blankney, and Metheringham, to Lincoln, where it joined the main line.

Another road, across the country from the salt mines in Worcestershire is supposed to have passed through the fens by Bolingbroke, Stickford, Sibsey, and so to Boston, and across the Witham by a ferry near Redstone Gowt, thence to Kirton and Donington, and so on in a straight line till it joined the branch above-described. The remains of this road may be clearly traced in the Bridge-end causeway, and by a foundation of stone and gravel which has been laid bare throughout its course; as also by milestones, one of which, near the Pincushion inn at Wyberton, remained in existence until quite recently.

The land, thus embanked, drained, and provided with roads, soon became fertile and covered with vegetation and trees, which appear from the remains that have been discovered to have flourished more vigorously in those days than they have under the more recent reclamation. Besides thus affording employment and subsistence to the Roman colonist, this part of the country doubtless also provided materials for export to the mother country, both manufactured and in their natural state. Of the latter kind, some of the British oysters, which were held in such great esteem by the epicures of the imperial city, were probably taken from their beds in the "Metaris Estuarim," known in modern days as Boston Deeps; and of the former it is supposed by some antiquaries that the salt pans, the remains of which have been discovered on many parts of this coast, are due to the art and industry of the Romans. The practice of manufacturing salt, by evaporating sea water in pans or reservoirs dug on the margin of a tidal stream, is exceedingly ancient, and the known skill and ability with which the Romans availed themselves of every opportunity of turning to good account the gifts of nature, may fairly lead us to suppose that they would adopt so simple a means of providing themselves with a supply of a commodity as valuable and scarce as salt was in those days. It is certain from the mention in many old Saxon chronicles of the numerous grants of land in which salt pans are mentioned, that their successors knew of this method of making salt, and that it was highly prized by them, great quantities being used for salting meat for their winter store of food.

After an occupation of upwards of 400 years, about the year A.D. 420, the Romans were obliged to withdraw their legions from Britain to assist in the defence of their own country. The same cause that effected the decline and fall of the Roman empire led to the occupation of this island by uncultivated and warlike Saxons. The movement amongst the Teutonic Nations of central Europe, which scattered them in all directions in quest of plunder and conquest, while leading the great body of that nation to the rich booty to be obtained in the cities of Italy, also sent the Saxons across the water to the neighbouring shores of Britain, which, deprived of its protectors, fell an easy prey to their predatory bands. Having once conquered the island they permanently settled here.

The Fens, lately so flourishing, soon became once more a scene of desolation. Tradition says that the Saxons, in their contests with the Britains, cut the banks and drowned the land on purpose; but even if this were not wilfully done, it is easy to conceive how soon the banks and sluices would go to decay and ruin, if neglected, and how rapidly the whole fen would become a mere morass covered daily by the tides, if they were not kept up. That no such attention and vigilance would be bestowed on them by the invaders we can easily conceive by the knowledge that history gives us of their character and barbarous habits at the time of their incursion. While the rudest dwellings sufficed to content them, war and plunder, perpetual quarrels and fights, occupied all their time; and while it is doubtful if they were possessed of knowledge and skill sufficient to maintain the engineering works constructed by their predecessors, it is certain they would hold in contempt the arts and practice of agriculture, for which purpose alone the fens were adapted.

For 200 years after the departure of the Romans the waters were allowed to have full dominion over the fens. The rivers, obstructed in their outfalls, prevented the rain-fall from flowing away, and the water, stagnating on the ground, made the whole a vast morass; the coarse grasses and herbage that sprang up in the summer months decayed away in the winter, and assisted in forming that layer of peat which is found more or less throughout the whole surface of the fens, but much deeper in the upper part, or that furthest removed from the sea. The eruption of the tides, through the broken banks, swept away at once all the signs of former prosperity, and the numerous trees, washed up by the roots, that have been found buried in the fen soil, attest to the power with which the torrent of waters devastated the land. Thus while the upland waters assisted in raising the surface by the formation of peat, the tides brought in a great quantity of silt and alluvial soil, which was deposited to a depth of from 12 to 18 feet at the parts near the mouths of the rivers, gradually diminishing towards the interior and higher grounds to a depth of from one to three feet. Numerous discoveries which have been made in excavations at different times in all parts of the Great Level bear witness to the correctness of this theory as to the formation of the upper stratum of the fens, of which the following are selected as samples:—In the excavations made for the erection of the Black Sluice, at Boston, in 1847, the first 12 feet was found to be warp, formed by a deposit of a reddish brown clay, left evidently by the sea; this rested on another layer of warp, five feet in thickness; which was followed by a stratum of peat 12 to 18 inches in thickness, in which were contained the remains of oak and other trees; below the peat was a layer of sand, and below this was the clay found everywhere beneath the fens, and which has been bored through, in Boston, to a depth of 555 feet. A well sunk at Sutton displayed a similar stratification; the first 16 feet was clayey warp, then came 3 to 4 feet of moor or peat; then 20 feet of soft moor mixed with shells and silt; then, for a distance of 95 feet, clay mixed with chalk stones; and below that gravel.

In digging for the foundations of the Grand Sluice, Boston, in 1764, at about 18 feet below the surface, the roots of several trees standing as they had grown were found; and also at about the same depth, a layer of shells of a kind similar to those found in the marsh creeks at the present time. In the excavations for Maud Foster sluice, in Skirbeck, there was found at 16 feet below the surface a smith's forge with all the tools belonging to it. In 1696, on the Welland, about 10 feet below the surface, the remains of old tan vats were discovered, and great quantities of horns and shoe soles of strange and unusual forms ; also a number of boats. (*Elstob's History of the Bedford Level.*) At Lynn a cart wheel was found 16 feet below the surface. In other parts of the fens great trees, swarths of grass, and other indications of cultivation have been found buried in silt and warp. While thus those discoveries clearly show that the surface has been raised near the outfalls of the rivers to a height of from 10 to 18 feet, the remains of trees, &c., crop up nearer to the surface the further they are removed from the coast. Thus at Bardney, Mr. Edwards in his survey in 1769 gives the following account of the formation of the ground :—" Bodiam sands, near Bardney, lie about three feet and a half below the surface of the adjacent lands. They consist of a thin bed of sand upon a bed of strong blue clay, full of large coggles and stones, on which bed was found a great number of oak, yew, and alder roots and trees which had grown thereon. The soil on each side is moory and full of subterranean wood to three and a half feet thick. The oak roots stand upon the sand, and tap-root in the clay. Some of the trees are five feet in diameter at the boll, and more than ten feet from out to out at the root." One large tree was discovered at Bardney containing 1440 feet of timber. This tree was found three feet below the surface, lying upon clay and gravel, and covered with peat. In Friskney, Wainfleet, and Wrangle, and in the East Fen, great numbers of fir trees with their roots have been discovered in the moory soil, one foot below the surface in the low parts, and from two to six feet in the higher lands. They lie in all directions, and appear to have been torn up by the operation of water.

In the excavations for the foundation of the engines and sluice now being constructed at Lade Bank, in the East Fen, at four feet below the surface a layer of peat about six inches in thickness was exposed: below this was three feet of soft blue clay, and then again a layer of peat with pieces of trees buried in it. This last layer rested on a bed of hard clay interspersed with chalk stones, and this continued as far as the borings extended, about thirty feet below the surface.

From the formation of the soil and these discoveries, it is evident that the whole surface of the fens must have been considerably raised by decaying vegetation and aqueous deposits spread over a long series of years. The trees prove that this deposit took place after the land had been protected from the salt water; and the shoe soles, smith's forge, and other articles of civilised life all denote a period posterior to the occupation of the island by the Romans.

The first returning signs of prosperity probably date from a period of 200 years after the departure of the Romans, when Pope Gregory, touched by the beauty of the fair complexion and blooming countenances of some English youths exposed for sale in the streets of Rome, and finding their native religion was that of Paganism, expressed his conviction that it was a pity that the prince of darkness should enjoy so fair a prey, and that so beautiful a frontispiece should cover minds destitute of internal grace and righteousness. He therefore sent St. Augustine, with forty other monks, to spread the knowledge of Christianity amongst the Saxons and Britons; and so successful was their mission that the doctrines of Christianity soon became deeply rooted throughout the whole of England. *(Hume's History of England)*. Amongst other monks who followed the footsteps of St. Augustine was one Guthlac, a holy man of God, who, seeking a place more desolate than any other whereto he might retire and pursue his holy meditations, came to Crowland, and finally settled there. His reputation for holiness soon attracted other monks, and ultimately a monastery was

c

established. The fens around are described by his biographer "as immense marshes, now a black pool of water, now foul running streams, and also many islands and reeds and hillocks, and with manifold windings, wide and long, it continues up to the North Sea." The fenny nature of the soil gave this place its name, as the meaning of the word is "crude" and "muddy" land. Crowland soon became a place of note in the kingdom, and about the year 716 Ethelbald, king of the Mercians, having been instructed by the counsels and prevailed upon by the prayers of the devout anchorite Guthlac, his dearly-beloved confessor, gave, granted, and delivered unto Almighty God and the blessed Virgin and Saint Bartholomew out of his demesnes, for the purpose of founding a monastery of black monks, the whole island of Crowland, the same to be set apart for the site of an abbey; and also granted from his treasury the sum of £300 towards the building of the same, and an annual payment of £100, with liberty to the monks to enclose as much of the marsh land as they should see fit. Other monasteries were established by the Saxons on the Witham. St. Botolph, in the year 654, built one on a desert piece of ground, near its mouth, supposed to be the site of the present town of Boston, and another was established at Bardney about the year 697. Saint Guthlac became the patron saint of the fens, and the numerous churches that are dedicated to his memory attest the esteem and popularity of the first Christian reclaimer of this part of England. In a niche in the wall of the parish church of Fishtoft is a statue of St. Guthlac, its patron saint; and there is a tradition connected with this statue that so long as the whip, the usual insignia of the saint, remained in his hand, the parish of Fishtoft should not be infested with rats and mice. *(Thompson's History).*

A love of desolation and seclusion, the old Chronicles tell us, was St. Guthlac's motive in seeking the fens for his residence.

His followers probably were attracted by other motives, amongst which may have been the valuable fisheries to be found in the fen rivers, which, anterior to their coming, had been of little benefit to the natives, for we are informed that the Saxons learnt the art of catching fish from the Romans. The art once acquired, fish became such a favorite food that the supply never equalled the demand. Turner, in his History of the Anglo-Saxons, thus refers to the value of fisheries:—" The Saxons eat various kinds of fish, but of this description of food the species that is most profusely noticed is the eel. They used eels as abundantly as swine. Two grants are mentioned, each yielding one thousand eels, and by another 2000 were received as an annual rent; 4000 eels were an annual present from the monks of Ramsey to those of Peterboro'. We read of two places, purchased for £21, wherein 16,000 of these fish were caught every year; and in one charter twenty fishermen are stated to have furnished during the same period 60,000 eels to the monastery." In the dialogues composed by Elfric to instruct the Anglo-Saxon youths, giving an account of the fisheries, the following are mentioned as forming the food of the people: eels, haddocks, skate, lampreys, and whatever swims in the river; and as the products of the sea, herrings, salmon, porpoises, sturgeons, oysters and crabs, mussels, cockles, and such like. Both the Witham and Welland were celebrated for their fish, and doubtless afforded many a dainty meal to the abstemious abbots and monks residing in the various establishments founded on their banks.

Mr. Morton, in his History of the Lincolnshire Churches, remarks: " It must not be supposed that monasteries were always places of corrupted morals. On their first introduction their members were laborious men who drained marshes, cleared woods, cultivated wastes, and protected the country from the wolves, then numerous." A colony of monks, in small numbers at first, transported themselves into some uncultivated place, and there, as missionaries and labourers at once, in the midst of a people as yet pagan, they accomplished their double task with as much of danger as of toil.

As these monasteries increased in size and importance, they attracted numerous retainers and servants, and attention would be given by the owners of the abbey lands to the improvement of the fens around. The establishment of Mercia, in which Lincolnshire was included, into a separate kingdom about this time, and its consequent prosperity, would also assist in the restoration of the fens to some degree of their former prosperity. In the year 870, the marshes, as they were then termed, are described by Hugo Candidus as furnishing wood and turf for fire, hay for cattle, reeds for thatching, and fish and water fowl for subsistence.

A temporary stop was put to this growing prosperity by the Danes, who in their various predatory incursions into England selected this part of the east coast as their favourite landing place. The following account of the invasion of the fens, by the Danes, in the year 870, the fourth of their residence in England, is given by Sharon Turner:—

"They embarked on the Humber, and sailing to Lincolnshire landed at Humberston, in Lindsey. After destroying the monastery, and slaying all the monks of Bardney, they employed the summer in desolating the country around with sword and fire. About Michaelmas they passed the Witham, and entered the district of Kesteven. The Earl Algar drew out the youth of Holland: his two seneschals, Wilbert and Leofric, assembled from Deeping, Langtoft, and Baston, 300 valiant and well-appointed men; 200 more joined him from Croyland monastery: they were composed of fugitives, and led by Tolius, who had assumed the cowl, but who, previous to entering the sacred profession, had been celebrated for his military character. Morcar, lord of Brunne (Bourne), added his family, who were undaunted and numerous. Osgot, the sheriff of Lincoln, collected 500 more from the inhabitants of the country. These patriots, not 3000 in number, united in Kesteven, with the daring hope of checking by their valour the progress of the ferocious invaders. On the feast of St. Maurice they attacked the advanced bands of the north men with such conspicuous bravery that they slew three of their kings and many of their soldiers : they chased the rest to the gates of their entrenchments, and notwithstanding a fierce resistance they assailed these till the advance of night compelled the valiant Earl to call off his noble army. The English, ultimately beaten, the Danes burned and destroyed all the towns and villages,—ravaged and destroyed Croyland Abbey ; the venerable Abbot was hewed down at the altar, and the Prior and the rest of the monks murdered ; all the tombs and monuments broken, and the ' superb edifice' devoured by fire ; having accomplished which they set out for Peterborough. The Danes were finally defeated in 878, and Alfred the Great re-ascended the throne of England. The monks returned to their ruined homes, which they soon set about re-building, and although during the intervening period of the Norman Conquest several incursions were made by the Danes, in which the fen men were engaged, no special fact is recorded by history which throws any light on the state and condition of the fens during this period."

On the floor of the chancel of Algarkirk Church is a monument on which is carved the full length figure of a man in alto-relievo, which Stukely states to be that of the Earl Algar here mentioned, and from whom the Parish takes its name.

At the time of and subsequent to the Conquest of the Island by William of Normandy, the fens became the refuge of the discontented Saxons ; or as Dugdale puts it, "This land is environed with fens and reed plecks—unpassable ; so that they feared not the invasion of an enemy, and in consequence of the strength of this place by reason of the said water encompassing it, divers of the principal nobility of the English nation had recourse into it as their greatest refuge against the strength and power of the Norman Conqueror." The fenny districts of the kingdom of Mercia had always been a country difficult to conquer, and the habitation of a people still more difficult to keep in subjection ; and these districts now became the 'camps of refuge' to the scattered and discomfited Saxons. When William the Conqueror had subdued all the rest of England, a brave body of men in the fens still refused him allegiance : their remote situation and solitary habits made them conservative of their ancient rights and privileges, and zealous in their allegiance to their liege lords and masters. " It is men of this kind, whose position gives them more natural security than their neighbours, and consequently more independence, who have been found the last to be conquered in every country where their subjugation has been attempted. What the rock and defile were to the mountaineer, the reed field and mere were to the fen man—his home, the source of his subsistence, and his defence in seasons of oppression or misfortune." Under Hereward, son of Leofric, Lord of Bourne, many a bold fight was made for liberty against the usurpers. Ivo of Taillebois, William of Ghent, and other Normans, to whom King William had given the land of the Saxons; and driven by the conquerors from place to place they at last made the Isle of Ely their final camp of refuge, where were collected many of the principal Saxon nobility and ecclesiastics. Long and nobly did Hereward, by his sagacity, bravery, and self-devotedness baffle all the attempts of the Normans to obtain possession of the stronghold. The deeds of Hereward long lived in the traditions of the people, and have come down to our day in the narratives of the ancient chronicles, and have lately been revived by a modern writer in the graphic and touching romance of Hereward the last of the English *(C. Kingsley)*, in which the writer shows a knowledge of the old fen country in Saxon times, such as only one who had studied the old chronicles could give. One short quotation from this interesting work may here be given, as descriptive of the fen country between Bourn and Crowland.

"Hereward had just returned from Flanders to his native country, and arriving at Bourne, the home of his ancestors, he finds the place besieged, and on enquiring what has happened is answered, 'What has happened makes free Englishmen's blood boil to tell of. Here, Sir Knight, three days ago, came in this Frenchman with some twenty ruffians of his own, and more of one Taillebois too to see him safe; says that this new King, this base-born Frenchman, has given away all Earl Morcar's lands, and that Bourne is his; kills a man or two; upsets the women; gets drunk, raffles, and roysters; breaks into my lady's bower, calling her to give up her keys, and when she gives them will have all her jewels too. She faces them like a brave Princess, and two of the hounds lay hold of her, and say that she shall ride through

Bourne as she rode through Coventry. The boy Godwin—he that was the great Earl's godson, our last hope—draws sword on them, and he, a boy of 16 summers, kills them both out of hand; the rest set on him, cut his head off, and there it sticks on the gable spike to this hour.' Hereward, enraged beyond endurance by this and other accounts of the evils that had fallen on his country, his family, and his friends, rushed down to the hall, where were assembled the Frenchmen engaged in drunken revelry, and with his own hand slays the whole of the guard left in charge of Bourne, fourteen in number. The next day he set out for Crowland Abbey with his mother, the Princess Godiva, and they went down to the water and took barge, and laid the corpse of young Godwin therein; and they rowed away for Crowland by many a mere and many an ea; through narrow reaches of clear brown glassy water; between the dark green alders; between the pale green reeds, where the boot clanked and the bittern boomed, and the sedge bird, not content with its own sweet song, mocked the song of all the birds around; and then out into the broad lagoons, where hung motionless high over head hawk beyond hawk, buzzard beyond buzzard, kite beyond kite, as far as the eye could see. Into the air as they rowed on whirred up the great skeins of wild fowl innumerable, with a cry as of all the bells of Crowland, or all the hounds of Bruneswold; and clear above all the noise sounded the wild whistle of the curlews, and the trumpet note of the great white swan; out of the reeds, like an arrow, shot the peregrine, singled one luckless mallard from the flock, caught him up, struck him stone dead with one blow of his terrible heel, and swept his prey with him into the reeds again."

The King having at last subdued Ely, the fen men, in common with the rest of England, had to submit to the conquering arm of William of Normandy, and the country was parcelled out amongst his followers, the land in this district being chiefly shared by Allan Rufus, Earl of Brittany and Richmond, Walter D'Eincourt, Guy de Creon or Croun, and Gilbert de Gaunt. The Earl of Brittany had his chief residence at Kirton, and there is reason to suppose that the Earl of Richmond had a seat in the parish of Boston, prior to the thirteenth century. Walter D'Eincourt also had a residence at Kirton, although the head of his barony was at Blankney; Guy de Croun resided at Freiston. And so the Norman blood became mingled with that of the Saxons of the fens, as the old Girvii, men of "Gyras"—a word which signifies a "deep fen"— had already crossed with the blood of Scandinavian Vikings in

Canute's conquest; and mixed with the descendants of Britons and invading Romans and Danes, and afterwards with French refugees, Huguenots from the persecutions of the Catholics. Vermuyden's Dutchmen again added the characteristics of another land, and left behind them marks of their country's manner that may yet be traced.

In Cromwell's time a number of Scotch prisoners, from the battle of Dunbar, and also Dutchmen taken in the naval engagement, in which Admiral Blake gained his glorious victory over the Dutch Admiral Van Tromp, were sent to work on the dykes and banks, many of whom settled down, and their descendants remain to the present day. To this strong intermixture of races, representing enterprising colonists, daring robbers, fierce soldiers, zealots who preferred expatriation to an abandonment of their particular tenets, the clean and steady Hollander, and the clear-headed and enterprising Scotchman, may be attributed that sturdy independence and self help, that freedom of thought and persevering industry and enterprise, which distinguish the inhabitants of the fens at the present day.

After the Norman Conquest, and the settlement of the island, the religious establishments began greatly to multiply, and many of these were settled in the fen country, which was described as " being full of monasteries, and as having large bodies of monks settled on the islands of these waters " *(William of Malmesbury)*; to whom were made grants of lands and rights of fishing, fowling, and turbary (digging turfs), which appear to have been considered of much value from the numerous disputes respecting these rights of which records exist. But although the idea of draining and reclaiming the fens was from time to time projected, and John of Gaunt Duke of Lancaster, who resided at Bolingbroke Castle, upon the borders of the fens, and who held considerable property within the level, and Margaret Countess of R} throu d took the matter in hand, nothing was actually done, and the chronicles inform us that " the generality of people in that age was possessed of an opinion that the project was utterly impossible to be brought about."

Besides the fisheries, the fens also afforded harbour and shelter to the wild animals of the country, and King Henry the First afforested all the low lands of South Lincolnshire, which continued for many years to be the King's hunting grounds. The game protected consisted of " wild fowls and beasts of the forest, as the hart, hind, and hare; of chase, as buck, doe, and fox; of warren, as rabbit, pheasant, and partridge."

The condition of the level seems to have been subject to constant changes; at one time presenting every appearance of prosperity, and being described " as a very paradise and a heaven for the beauty and delight thereof, the very marshes bearing goodly trees." *(William of Malmesbury.)* That it must have greatly increased in importance and prosperity is evidenced by the fact that in the year 1204 the town of Boston had grown into such importance as to have a charter granted to it by King John; and it carried on at that time the manufacture of woollen cloth to a considerable extent. In the same century Holland Fen was ordered to be divided into townships. On the other hand there are frequent accounts of floods, and complaints of bad drainage. In 1281 Holland Fen was inundated, and in 1288 great part of Boston was drowned; and Henry III., taking notice that not only the land owners in those parts but himself had suffered considerable damage by the overflowing of the sea, and also of the fresh waters through default in the repair of the banks, sewers, and ditches, directed the shirereeve to distrain the goods of all land-owners who ought to have repaired the banks and scoured out the drains. And in the following reign commissioners were appointed to view the banks and sewers, and to see that the ancient passages of the waters were kept open and the banks properly repaired. From this time forward numerous commissions were issued by the Crown for the like purpose, until the establishment of the Court of Sewers in the reign of King Henry VIII.

Neglect was not the only cause which led to the inundation of the fens, for in the year 1335 one Rodger Pedwardine was accused of having cut the sea and river banks, and thereby inundated the low country. The struggle between the waters of the sea and the protecting works of man were constant and of varied success, and many a tale of devastation and ruin could be narrated from broken banks and an inundated country. One of the earliest since the Conquest that is recorded was 1178, when the old sea bank broke, and the whole fen country was deluged by the sea. Similar floods occurred in 1236, 1254, and 1257; and in 1287, through the vehemency of the wind and the violence of the sea, the monastery of Spalding and many churches were overthrown and destroyed. "All the whole country in the parts of Holland were for the most part turned into a standing pool, so that an intolerable multitude of men, women, and children were overwhelmed with the water, especially in the town of Boston, a great part whereof was destroyed." *(Stow's Chronicle.)* Again in 1467 a very serious flood occured, a calamity of some kind having previously been prognosticated by extraordinary appearances in the air, which are described by Ingulphus with great minuteness, who is entitled to undoubted credence from the fact of an examination having been made into the subject before no less a personage than the Lord Archbishop of Canterbury. The same historian tells us "that there was scarcely a house or building but what the waters made their way and flowed through it; and this remained continuously during a whole month, the waters either standing there without flowing off, or else, being agitated by strong gusts of wind, swelled and increased still more and more day after day. Nor on this occasion did the embankments offer any effectual resistance, but on the contrary, though materials had been brought from other quarters for the purpose of strengthening them, they proved of very little service for that purpose. However diligently the work might have been attended to in the day time, as the water swelled and rose, the spot under repair was completely laid bare during the night." *(Ingulphus.)*

A century later, in the reign of Queen Elizabeth, another serious flood occurred, on the 5th of October, 1571 : owing to a violent tempest of wind and rain the whole country was flooded. An immense number of ships were wrecked on the coast. Churches and buildings were swept away, and many lives lost. At Mumby Chapel the whole town was lost, except three houses; and the church was wholly overthrown except the steeple. A ship was driven upon a house, the sailors saving themselves by clinging to the roof; and the narrative adds to the romance by telling us that " the sailors thought they had bin upon a rocke committed themselves to God; and three of the mariners lept out from the shippe and chaunced to take hold of the house toppe, and so saved themselves; and the wife of the same lying in childbed did climb up into the top of the house, and was also saved by the mariners, her husband and child being both drowned." Holland, Leverington, Long Sutton, and Holbeach were all overflown, and many sheep, oxen, and horses were drowned. Bourne was overflowed to the midway of the height of the church. This calamity extended over many counties, and did an enormous amount of harm. *(Hollingshed.)*

At the end of the last and the beginning of the present century, several very high tides occurred which did much damage. On the 1st of January, 1779 a heavy gale of wind caused the tide to flow unusually high, doing damage in Boston and the neighbourhood. On the 19th October, 1801, and on November 30th,

1807, high tides occurred, which flowed so high as to deluge the streets of Boston and inundate the houses; and the latter tide caused the water to rise so high as to enter the church and flow as far as the pulpit. The extraordinary high tide of the 10th of November, 1810, was attended by the most calamitous results, arising from a breach of the sea banks in several places along the coast. The following account of the effects of this tide is given by a modern writer :—

"The whole of the day was very rainy and tempestuous; the wind blew impetuously from the E.S.E., and gradually increased in violence till the evening, when it became a perfect hurricane. The consequence of this continued gale was, that the evening tide came in with great rapidity, and rose to an unprecedented height, being 4½ inches higher than that of November, 1807; whole streets in the vicinity of the river were completely inundated; and many parts of the town, which had hitherto escaped the effects of a high tide, were on this occasion covered to a considerable depth with water. Owing to the sea banks having given way in many parts of the neighbourhood; and an immense quantity of water having spread itself through the breaches over the adjacent country, which on the ebb of the tide had to return the same way until it reached their level, the water in the streets of Boston did not perceptibly abate for nearly an hour. The old sea banks were insufficient, and the surge dashed over them for nearly their whole extent and in its fall scoured away the soil of the bank on the land side from the summit to the base, by which means breaches were occasioned. The whole extent of country, from Wainfleet to Spalding, shared in this calamity; great numbers of sheep and other cattle were drowned; corn and haystacks were swept away, and property to the following amount destroyed : Individual losses, £16,810 10s.; injury to public sea banks, £3500; injury to private sea banks, £8000; total, £28,310 10s. A subscription was entered into to relieve in some degree the distress of those who had been injured by this great calamity." (*Thompson's History of Boston.*)

The sea banks were repaired, strengthened, and heightened, and afterwards again tested by another high tide on the 2nd of March, 1820, which proved disastrous to the private banks enclosing the out-marshes from Butterwick to Wainfleet, but the repairs of the old sea banks saved them from material injury.

Extraordinary high tides occurred in August, 1866 and December, 1867, but the highest since that of 1810 was on the 8th of February last, when the whole of the eastern coast was visited by a remarkably high tide, caused by strong westerly gales blowing the water out of the Atlantic, and a sudden change to the N.E., driving it on this coast. Fortunately the spring tides were not at their height until three days after this occurred, or the damage done would have been more serious than it was. The lands on the Humber and the Ouze suffered most severely, the banks being broken in several places; but the effect in flooding houses and destroying property was severely felt in every river from the Tyne to the Thames and the Medway. This tide rose to a height of 24¼ feet above the cill of Hobhole sluice,—which is level with low water, of spring tides in Clayhole, in the Estuary—or within 21 inches of the tide of 1810. The effect of the wind on the action of the tides was shown in a remarkable way by this occurrence, the tide of the previous evening being nearly six feet lower, and that of the following evening three feet lower.

By so precarious a tenure is the fen land held, and so great is the necessity for constant and unremitting vigilance and care, that with the least neglect, only perhaps an unseen rat hole, the waving corn fields are turned into a sea of water. So important has everything that is conducive to the preservation of these banks been deemed by the Legislature of the country that in the Game Act special exception is made in their favour, and any person is at liberty to shoot or destroy the rabbits or conies found on any sea bank on the Lincolnshire coast. The laws in olden times were very stringent as to the preservation of the banks. Swine were not allowed to go upon them, unless they were ringed, under a penalty of one penny—equal to a shilling in our money;—in case of a breach the sheriff was authorised to impress diggers and laborers for repairing the embankments. A terrible penalty for neglect is mentioned by Harrison, in his preface to *Hollingshed's Chronicles*, who says that " Such as having walls or banks, near unto the sea, and do suffer the same to decay, after convenient admonition, whereby the water entereth and drowneth up the country, are by a certain ancient custom apprehended, condemned, and *staked in the breach*, where they remain for ever a parcel of the new wall that is to made upon them as I have heard reported."

Yet important as the preservation of these ramparts are to the security of the country, perhaps little thought is given by the occupier of the land as he pursues his daily calling as to how much he owes to these works of the ancient Romans. Custom makes all things common; and yet when the danger comes the sturdy independence and self help, so characteristic of the fen men, is called forth to the fullest extent.

"No one has ever seen a fen bank break without honouring the stern quiet temper which there is in the fen men, when the north-easter is blowing above, the spring tide roaring outside, the brimming tide-way lapping up to the dyke top, or flying over in sheets of spray; when round the one fatal thread which is trickling over the dyke, or worse, through some forgotten rat's hole in its side, hundreds of men are clustered, without tumult, without complaint, marshalled under their employers, fighting the brute powers of nature, not for their employers' sake alone, but for the sake of their own year's labour, and their own year's bread. The sheep have been driven off the land below; the cattle stand ranged shivering on high dykes inland: they will be saved in punts, if the worst befall, but a hundred spades, wielded by practised hands, cannot stop that tiny rat hole. The trickle becomes a rush, the rush a roaring waterfall. The dyke top trembles—gives. The men make efforts, desperate dangerous, as of sailors in a wreck, with faggots, hurdles, sedge turf; but the bank will break, and slowly they draw off, sullen, but uncomplaining; beaten but not conquered. A new cry arises among them. Up, to save yonder sluice; that will save yonder lode; that again yonder farm: that again some other lode, some other farm, far back inland, but guessed at instantly by men who have studied from their youth, as the necessity of their existence, the labyrinthine drainage of lands which are all below the water level, and where the inner lands in many cases are lower still than those outside.

"So they hurry away to the nearest farms; the teams are harnessed, the waggons filled, and drawn down and emptied; the beer cans go round cheerily, and the men work with a sort of savage joy at being able to do something, if not all, and stop the sluice on which so much depends. As for the outer land it is gone past hope; through the breach pours a roaring salt cataract, digging out a hole on the inside of the bank, which remains as a deep sullen pond for years to come. Hundreds, thousands of pounds are lost already, past all hope. Be it so then. At the next neap tide perhaps they will be able to mend the dyke, and pump the water out; and begin again, beaten but not conquered, the same everlasting fight with wind and wave which their forefathers have waged for now 1800 years." (*C. Kingsley.*)

From the time of the Norman Conquest till the reign of James the First, the fens remained as common land, the monasteries and religious houses having certain rights of pasturage and turbary. After the dissolution of the monasteries by Henry VIII. these rights fell into the hands of numerous private individuals, and were the occasion of many disputes, the records of which exist in the annals of the law courts. Commissions were issued to settle the boundaries of the fens, and determine the rights of the Crown; and in Queen Elizabeth's reign a code of fen laws, for the regulation of the commoners, was issued, to which a fuller mention will be made hereafter. The attempts made by the Earl of Bedford to reclaim the great Bedford Level directed the attention of King James to the state of the other fens in Lincolnshire, and many efforts were made through the Court of Sewers to improve the drainage; but owing to the inability of this court to compel the payment of taxes necessary for carrying out the work, the various schemes fell through, and were otherwise postponed, in consequence of the unsettled state of the country during the civil wars. In the reign of Charles the First grants were made of these fens to certain "undertakers," who in consideration of their having a portion of the land granted to them as their reward, undertook to reclaim the land; and to a great extent succeeded; but in the lawless times that followed they found it impossible to preserve their possessions from the attacks of the dispossessed fen men, who cut the banks, pulled up the sluices, and threw down the dykes. And so the fens remained in a partial state of reclamation till the year 1762, when an Act was obtained for the improvement of the low lands on the Witham. Under the power of this Act the river was improved, and the Grand Sluice erected at Boston. This was followed by an Act for the better drainage and reclamation of Holland Fen and the Black Sluice district in 1765. The Act for the enclosure of the East and West Fens dates from 1801, and for Deeping Fen about the same time, steam power being applied in 1823.

The general principle on which the drainage of the fens is laid out is that of gravitation, large arterial drains being cut through the centre of the fens, protected by self-acting doors to exclude the tides, at their junction with the main river. These large drains are fed by a complete network of smaller sewers, which ramify throughout the whole of the level, and conduct the rainfall from the land to the main drains, and through them to the sea.

The same error has been committed in the drainage of these fens as Sir Cornelius Vermuyden fell into in laying out that of the Bedford Level. The whole attention of the various undertakers and commissioners has been applied to the improvement of the interior drainage, and the outfall has been entirely neglected. The scheme carried out by Sir C. Vermuyden consisted in making a great number of new straight cuts in the interior of the level, and shutting out the tidal waters from these by means of sluices. Unfortunately he had drawn his conclusions from his knowledge of Holland and Flanders. These countries were utterly dissimilar to the fens of the counties of Lincoln and Cambridge. The former were contiguous to the sea, and recovered directly from it, and were unprovided with any natural rivers, rendering the use of sluices absolutely necessary. The fens of this part of the country are several miles from the ocean, and through their midst run natural rivers which at one time had regular and continued currents. Vermuyden was opposed at the time by Westerdyke, a countryman of his own, and by others, who pointed out the natural and obvious course to pursue, that is to begin at the outfall and to scour out, straighten, widen, and deepen the main rivers and embank their sides, and then to have cut off the high land waters with catch-water drains as the Romans had done before, and as Rennie did afterwards. This done, the completion of the interior drainage would have been comparatively a simple and easy undertaking. Instead of pursuing this course, Vermuyden utterly neglected his outfalls; in many cases abandoned the natural rivers and devoted his whole energies to the interior drainage, expending the capital of his employers in making long straight cuts and sluices, which afterwards were found ineffectual because they could not void the waters which drained into them, owing to the outfall being rendered defective by neglect and the operations of these very works. (*Well's History of the Bedford Level.*) Badeslade, in his account of the Great Level, remarks that if the fens had been provided with proper drains to convey their downfall waters into the great rivers, and if art had been applied to assist nature in embanking these instead of contradicting her by erecting sluices, nature would have kept the outfalls so wide and deep that the fens would have been perfectly drained. It will be seen, as this history proceeds, that nearly the whole of the level of the fens here treated of, is capable of being drained by natural means if only the outfall be properly protected, and the rivers allowed to act in the way nature intended them by the free flux and reflux of the tides; and that this is no mere theory of the author, but is the expressed opinion of every engineer of eminence who has been called in to advise on the drainage. Unfortunately the engineers have had to yield their opinions to those of their employers, and consequently mechanical means have to be adopted at great and continuous expense to do that which nature would willingly do for us if only she were properly assisted by art.

The water falling on the lands lying below the ordinary height of flood level was in the first instance lifted up by means of wheels worked by wind mills. The origin of the introduction of wind mills as applied to drainage is said to have arisen from the necessity that the engineers of the Bedford Level Commission found from time to time of employing some mechanical means of emptying the drains when requiring to be cleaned out. For this purpose, in the first instance, large scoops, so constructed as to be handled by a number of men, were used; but in 1687 the Corporation of the Bedford Level provided mills, consisting of a wheel with floats, very similar to the old breast wheel, to which motion was given by horses. In the year 1699 a person of the name of Green erected one of these mills at Slade to drain his land; and in 1703 another was erected by Silas Tytus. Both these were considered nuisances and ordered to be pulled down. The owners resorted for relief to a Court of Equity, but the termination of the suit was favorable to the Corporation.

Although from this it would appear that these mills were opposed to popular opinion, they made such advancement that they soon took their place as absolute necessities in the economy of drainage. The level had become so inundated by the choking up of the interior drains, the defective state of the rivers themselves, and the neglect to improve the outfalls to the sea, that the Corporation found it impossible to resist the importunity of the country to resort to an artificial system of interior drainage. (*Well's History of the Bedford Level*). In the year 1726 an Act was obtained for the effectual drainage of Haddenham Fen by the use of mills, and after this their use became general. Horsepower soon gave way to the wind, but the operations of this capricious element were found to be too uncertain, and a more expensive but effective substitute was found in steam. The largest engines in this district are those erected for the drainage of Deeping Fen in 1824, consisting of two engines of an aggregate power of 140 horses, and working two large scoop wheels, which lift the whole of the water from Deeping Fen, containing 25,000 acres. Numerous engines for the drainage of small tracts of land exist in different parts of the fens: those that have been in existence for some years work the old-fashioned scoop, but these are gradually giving way to the centrifugal pump.*

This reference to the mechanical appliances that have been brought into action in the drainage of the fens would not be complete without mention of the plan adopted for emptying the water from the Middle Level over the dam that was made to stay the tides at the fatal inundation that took place in 1861, by the blowing up of the Middle Level Sluice. In lieu of erecting steam pumps, Mr. Hawkshaw proposed that the principle of the syphon should be applied, and for this purpose 16 large bent tubes, each 150 feet long, and 3ft. 6in. in diameter, are placed on the embankment, with the short leg in the drain, and the long one in the river. Three air-pumps are attached to the syphons, and are used to exhaust the air from the tubes, being worked by a ten-horse-power engine. These syphons have, up to the present time, been found to perform their work satisfactorily, and have no doubt answered the purpose for which they were intended.

Further details of the works of drainage, and of the constitution of the various commissions who have the control over them, will be given in connection with the history of each fen. Suffice it here to say, in conclusion, that the reclamation of the fens, and their present wonderfully fertile condition, is due to the ingenuity and perseverance of their inhabitants, aided by the skill of the most talented engineers who have lived during the last hundred years. Nearly every engineer of high standing has

---

* The sketch at the end of this chapter is taken from a mill and drainage wheel still used for lifting the water off the land into one of the drains in Holland Fen.

left his mark on some part of this great level. Smeaton, Telford, Labelye, the designer of the old Westminster Bridge; Mylne, the builder of Blackfriars Bridge; the Rennies, Cubitt, Brunel, Walker, and Robert Stephenson, have all been called at various times; and even now it is only by the constant and vigilant attention of skilled men that the fens are preserved. The ruin and devastation, the long and costly litigation, and the ultimate heavy tax on the land, caused by the Middle Level inundation, is a sad instance of the serious consequences arising from neglect, and shows how dependent is the cultivation of the soil on the skill and attention of the engineer.

DRAINAGE MILL AND WHEEL.

CHAPTER II.

THE RIVER WITHAM AND THE FENS ADJACENT.

The river Witham takes its rise at the village of South Witham, about ten miles north of Stamford ; and after a circuitous course of about 68 miles empties itself into Boston Deeps. The shape of the river may be compared to a horseshoe, the upper part of the shoe being at Lincoln, and the two ends respectively at South Witham and Fishtoft, the distance between the two points being about 28 miles.

The Witham, springing at Thistleton and South Witham, thence flows almost due north, past Colsterworth, Great and Little Ponton, to Grantham, at each of which places it receives tributary streams. It then continues its northerly course past the beautiful grounds of Belton and Syston, whence it takes a westerly direction to Long Benington, receiving on its way the Honington Brook, and a stream one head of which rises in the vale of Belvoir and the other at Denton, and both united join the Witham at Hougham; whence it turns again north, and passes Claypole, Barnaby, Beckingham, Stapleford, Thurlby, and Hykeham. At the latter place another tributary joins it, having its rise near Caythorpe and Fulbeck ; and also at Welbourne, and continues through a wide sandy valley to Lincoln. Here its direction is changed eastward for about eight miles; and after receiving at this point another considerable stream turns south-east, and continues in that direction till it discharges its contents into Boston Haven. At Bardney, Stixwould, and Dogdyke it receives additions from small streams ; and at Tattershall the Bain discharges its waters, after a course of about 25 miles, having its rise at Ludford, and passing Horncastle and Scrivelsby on its way.

The length of the Witham, as already stated, is 68 miles. The total area of land drained by this river is about 680,392 acres, of which 414,988 acres are high lands, and 265,404 fens, or lands drained by artificial cuts. The history of the Witham may be traced back to very early times. There is reason for believing that during the time of the Romans, who had a station at Lincoln, and long afterwards, the Witham admitted ships of considerable size to sail thither, as remains of them have been discovered deeply buried by the accumulation of the deposit left by the waters. Dugdale mentions that large ribs of ships had, within memory, been there dug up, and this receives further confirmation from the following circumstance:—On digging for a foundation to build a house, at the upper end of the main street in Lincoln, a boat was discovered, which, by a chain and lock, was fastened to a post. *(Chapman's Facts and Remarks.)* This spot being many yards higher than the middle of that valley, through which the Witham runs, it is inferred that the boat had been moored at the side of the river and sunk and silted up, and that the channel must there have been both broad and deep.

In William the Conqueror's time Lincoln was one of the most important cities in England, and Leland tells us that men flocked there both by land and water; and in Henry the First's reign we are informed that Lincoln possessed a very large share of the import and export trade of the kingdom. In Edward the Third's reign it was made a staple for wool, leather, and lead. The Witham was the only source by which this trade could have been carried on, and must therefore have been in a condition navigable for ships of a size competent to cross the seas to foreign parts. It is even asserted that the bed of the river was considerably lower than it is now, and that the tide ran quite up to the city, and raised the water at the Swan-pool two or three feet. In 1743 it had so far deteriorated that spring tides only rose two feet six inches at the mouth of the river Bain.

The Witham, besides being a great highway to one of the most populous cities in England at that time, received additional importance from its fisheries. Camden says it was famous for its pike, hence the old saying, "Witham pike, England hath none the like." Another writer informs us that, owing to the abundance and quality of fish found in the fen rivers, the monks and holy men were led to choose situations near their banks for the erection of their religious houses. Right of fishery in this stream was granted by William de Gaunt in the year 1115 to the Abbey of Bardney; and in the year 1162 a fishery on the Witham, near Dogdyke, was given to the monks of Kirkstead by William de Kyme.

The religious establishments on the banks of the Witham were more numerous perhaps than those of any other river in Britain within the same compass. Twelve of these houses were erected within twenty miles, viz., at Monkshouse, Barlings, Bardney, Tupholme, Stixwould, Kirkstead, and Tattershall on the eastern side; and Kyme, Catley, Mere, Nocton, and Haverholme on the western. The holy residents of these establishments did not always behave in a manner that was to be expected from their calling. They did not follow out the golden rule of "doing to others as they would that others should do to them," for in the reign of Edward the First the holy nuns of Stixwould were accused of making an encroachment on the river, which operated to the serious injury of the country, and they were ordered to remove it.

The gradual extension of the population which gathered round these monasteries caused attention to be paid to the condition of the low lands on either side of the river between Lincoln and Boston, which were overflowed all the winter, necessitating constant attention to the river; the descent of the stream from Lincoln to the sea being so little, that the water having a slow passage, could not keep it wide and deep enough either for navigation or for draining the adjacent marshes without the frequent helps of digging and clearing the same. The earliest mention that is made of legislative interference for the management of this river was in Edward the Third's reign, when a presentment was made in the Court of King's Bench that, owing to the default of the town of Coningsby, the channel of the river in Wildmore was bending and defective, and consequently the marshes of Wildmore and Bolingbroke were overflowed and drowned.

In 1342 (16 Edw. III.) a petition was presented to the King, stating that the " Ea of Kyme," betwixt Doedyke and Brent Fen, was so obstructed by mud, &c., that ships laden with wine, wool, and other merchandise could not pass as they used to do. Towards the latter end of this reign the river was cleansed and widened by royal patent. In Richard the Second's reign a commission was appointed for the view and repair of those banks and sewers betwixt Hildike and Bolingbroke, and betwixt the river Witham and the sea, and to do all things therein according to the law and custom of this realm, and according to the custom of Romney Marsh ; and also to take so many diggers and labourers, upon competent salaries, in regard of the then urgent necessity as should be sufficient to accomplish that work. (*Dugdale.*)

Several other commissions were issued in subsequent reigns for the like purpose, and in Henry the Seventh's reign (1500) a Council was held to settle the best means to be taken to improve the river, at which they determined to send to Flanders for some experienced person to advise them. May Hake was the chosen engineer, and under his advice it was determined that a sluice should be erected across the river at Boston. A new commission was appointed, which was instructed to ascertain the number of acres ; order statute duty to be performed till the work was finished ; levy contributions: send ships to Calais for Hake and his companions skilled in embanking and draining, and for materials for the work; appoint proper officers for directing and expediting the same, and whatever else might fall under the necessary management of the concern. The sum of £1000 was borrowed for carrying out the work, until such time as it could be levied by the Commissioners of Sewers, according to the law of Romney Marsh. Hake was to be paid for his services at the rate of 4s. per week, with a gratuity of £50 on the successful completion of the work. The stonemasons and stonehewers, fourteen of whom he agreed to bring with him, were to have 4s. per week.

The sluice was accordingly erected. The situation appears to have been under or near the old wooden bridge over the Witham at Boston, as mention is subsequently made of a sluice there. It does not seem to have answered the expectation of the promoters, for towards the end of the 16th century the state of the river was worse than ever. The exact principle on which the sluice was constructed does not appear; but that it was not intended to exclude the tidal waters may be gathered from the fact that in the year 1700 spring tides are stated to have risen ten feet at a distance of five miles above Boston, and from a remark in a paper of one Dr. Browne, written about the year 1560, "That the sluice was not according to the first meaning and determination, but should have been made with a pair of fludd gates, that the fludd should have no further course than the bridge, but so to have returned back again; and the fresh water following the salt, which should continue fresh above the bridge, to have had at all times fresh water for the commodity of the town during the time of the fludd. And also to have scoured the haven daily both above the sluice and to the seaward."

From this time the river continued to decay, owing to the decline of the trade and commerce of Boston, by the withdrawal of certain merchants. And it seems probable that in consequence of the trade being lost, the motives to labour for the security of a country which could not vend its staple commodity, must have been few and feeble.

The suppression of the religious houses by Henry VIII. also tended very seriously to injure the drainage by the river; for their spiritual tenants were assiduous in preserving their property, and improving their lands by attending to the work of sewers, and it cannot be doubted that these would be neglected, and the drainage suffer when the King seized upon their revenues and banished the proprietors.

The fens adjacent to the Witham were, no doubt, included in the various schemes which were carried out in the reign of Charles the First, and attention directed to the state of the river; but no particular mention of this is made by Dugdale and other ancient writers on the subject. The attempts made for the reclamation of the East and West and Wildmore Fens will be detailed hereafter in a chapter devoted to their special history.

In the year 1720 the North Forty-foot Drain was constructed by Earl Fitzwilliam for the drainage of a tract of land belonging to him, lying to the north of Kyme Eau. Having made repeated applications, without success, to the Court of Sewers to drain his lands, he determined to undertake the work himself, and for that purpose cut the North Forty-foot, which, passing under Kyme Eau, discharged its waters at a new sluice erected a little above Boston bridge, and by this means withdrew from the Witham a great quantity of water which used to find its way into the river at the sluice at Langrick, much to the detriment of the channel above Boston, and very little to his own benefit, for it appears that so ineffectual was the new drainage that one of the tenants cut his own banks to rid himself of the water, and let it flow into Holland Fen.

About the beginning of the 18th century numerous breaches are reported as existing in the banks from neglect, through which the waters ran in and out of the fens; and the lands continued in a drowned state, and the navigation completely lost, till the year 1761. The means and powers at the disposal of the Court of Sewers, the body having the control over these fens, being found quite inadequate to carry out any general measure for their improvement, the proprietors most largely interested in the state of the land met together, and determined to apply to Parliament to supersede the Court of Sewers so far as this district was concerned, and to sanction the appointment of a new commission vested with considerable powers for levying taxes and performing works, and all other things for draining and reclaiming the fen and restoring the navigation. Mr. Langley Edwards being appointed engineer, under his advice a scheme for the improvement of the river was settled, and in the second year of George the Third was passed " An Act for draining and preserving certain low lands, lying on both sides of the river Witham, in the county of Lincoln, and for restoring and maintaining the navigation of the said river from the High-bridge, in the city of Lincoln, through the borough of Boston to the sea." (2 George III., c. xxxii.) The preamble to this Act recites, that the river Witham, in the county of Lincoln, was formerly navigable for lighters, barges, boats, and other vessels from the sea through Boston to the High-bridge, in the city of Lincoln; but by the sand and silt brought in by the tide the outfall thereof into the sea had, for many years last past, been greatly hindered and obstructed, and was then in a great measure stopped up, lost, and destroyed, and thereby great part of the low lands and fens lying on both sides of the said river (and which contain together about one hundred thousand acres) were frequently overflowed and rendered useless and unprofitable, to the great loss of the respective owners thereof, the decay of trade and commerce, and the depopulation of the country; and that in the judgment and opinion of experienced engineers and persons of known skill and ability, the navigation of the said river Witham, and the outfall thereof into the sea, were capable of being restored and maintained, and the said low lands and fens of being drained, cultivated, and improved, but that the same could not be done without the authority of Parliament.

The district now included in the Witham commission is that tract of land lying on either side of the river, extending from Lincoln on the north to the town of Boston on the south, stretching eastward as far as the higher grounds in Freiston, Butterwick, Bonington, Leake, Wrangle, and Frisknoy, and bounded on the west by the Cardyke, the old catchwater drain of the Romans, which separated the high lands from the fens. The East Fen was not included in the first Act, but was added in the year 1801. (41 George III. cap. 135.)

For the purposes of the Act the level was divided into six districts. The first, comprising the fens on the south-west side of the Witham, extending from Lincoln to Dogdyke, the second, Holland Fen and the adjoining lands, bounded by Dogdyke and Kyme Eau on the north, the Witham on the east, and south and west by Swineshead, Heckington, and Brothertoft; the third district comprised the fens on the north-east side of the Witham, stretching from Lincoln to Tattershall: the fourth district, the Wildmore and West and East fens; the fifth district, fens in Anwick, North Kyme, Ruskington, Dorrington, and Digby; the sixth, fens in South Kyme, Great Hale, Little Hale, Heckington, Ewerby, Howell, and Swineshead.

The General Commission was to consist of 37 members, 31 of whom were to be elected by the several districts in the following proportions:—The first were entitled to send 7 representatives, the second 6, the third 5, the fourth 8, the fifth 2, and the sixth 3. Each member elected must have qualified for the office by taking a prescribed oath, and must have been in possession of land of the value of £100 per annum, or personal property to the value of £2000, or be heir apparent to landed property of the value of £200 per annum. The remaining six members consisted of the Mayors of Boston and Lincoln for the time being, and two Commissioners elected by the city of Lincoln, and two by the borough of Boston. The Commissioners were to be elected every three years, but in default of such election taking place the old Commissioners were to remain in office. An annual meeting was to be held every year on the first Tuesday in July, at either Lincoln, Boston, or Sleaford. Each district had also its own commission for the management of the interior drainage works in their respective neighbourhood, the number of members being regulated by the number of parishes in each district, each parish electing one representative; and the qualification for a vote being the ownership of land liable to taxation of the value of £5, or an occupation of £50. These Commissioners elected from amongst themselves certain members, as before stated, to represent them at the Board of the General Commission, who had the control of all the arterial drains and outfall sluices, and a general supervision over the whole level.

A Navigation Commission was also appointed, separate from the Drainage Trust, consisting of the Mayor of Lincoln and four other members elected by the burgesses, the Mayor of Boston and four members elected by the Corporation, and ten members elected by the General Drainage Commissioners. The functions of this body were the restoration of the navigation; and for this purpose they had power to erect locks, make cuts, and clean out the rivers; and were to pay the extra expenses in providing a lock at the new sluice to be erected at Boston. To enable them to execute these works they were authorised to take tolls (not exceeding 1s. 6d. per ton) on all boats navigating the Witham, and to raise money on the security of the tolls. In pursuance of the powers so granted, the Commissioners expended £6,800 in deepening the river and building the new locks and other works, and once more made it navigable for vessels, but of a different class to those that sailed up the river on the flood tide to Lincoln, when that city was in its palmy days as a mercantile town.

The works for the improvement of the drainage sanctioned by this Act, and subsequently carried out, consisted of straightening the course of the river Witham by making a new cut from Boston to Chapel-hill, and cleansing, widening, and deepening the river from that place to Stamp-end, near Lincoln; the fishing weirs and other obstructions which had hitherto hindered the full course of the waters were removed; the sides of the river were embanked and the water prevented flowing on the adjacent lands, while its discharge was effected by the cleansing and deepening of the Kyme Eau, Billinghay Skirth, the Bane, and other tributaries and side drains. The new cut from Boston to Chapel-hill was laid out by the engineer in a direct line between those two places; but to oblige one large proprietor the channel was turned from its proper direction so as to run by Anton's Gowt; and to accommodate another, it was made to go off thence, at a sharp angle, towards Langrick. (*Chapman's Facts and Remarks.*) The dimensions of this cut, as set out in the Act, were 80 feet top and 50 feet bottom, the top diminishing to 68 feet at Chapel-hill, the depth being on an average 9 feet 6 inches.

At the lower end of the cut was erected a " Grand Sluice " for stemming the tide, on a piece of ground called Harrison's Four Acres, between Lodowick's Gowt and Boston bridge; the floor whereof was three feet at least lower than the floor of the said gowt, and its capacity, or clear water way, was fifty feet wide, with three pairs of pointing doors to the sea-ward, to shut with the flow of the tides (a fourth opening being built by the Navigation Commissioners), and also pointing frames, provided with drops, or draw doors, on the land side, to be shut occasionally in order to retain fresh water in dry seasons for the use of cattle and the navigation. The top of the draw doors being guaged to such a height as to retain the water of the river not higher, at ordinary seasons, than two feet below the medium surface of the lowest lands that drain therein. Act 2 Geo. III., chap. 32.*

A new sluice, of 14 feet water way, was also made at Anton's Gowt for the discharge of the water from the West and Wildmore Fens, having a pair of pointing doors towards the Witham to prevent the floods of that river backing on to the Fens. The sluice was connected with the former system of drainage by a new cut to the place where the old Anton's Gowt stood. The Commissioners were further empowered to build a bridge across the new cut, or river, at a point about half-way between Anton's Gowt and Boston, for the purpose of preserving the communication with the several lands of Boston West and Holland Fen. This part of the Act was never carried out.

The site of the new sluice was the subject of much contention between the Commissioners and the town of Boston; the latter being anxious that it should be erected in the place of the old bridge; but the Commissioners, apprehensive that the town would gain great advantage from its erection in that situation, while it would be disadvantageous to the drainage, selected a spot about a quarter of a mile above the bridge, and the same distance to to the east of the old river. The foundation-stone of the Grand Sluice was laid by Charles Amcotts, Esquire, on the 26th March, 1764; and it was opened by the engineer, Mr. Langley Edwards, on the 15th October, 1766, in the presence of a very large concourse of spectators, estimated as numbering ten thousand persons, amongst whom were many of the nobility and gentry from remote parts of the kingdom. The Sluice disappointed the

---

* The engraving of the Grand Sluice at the end of this chapter is from a photograph taken by Mr. Hackford for the author.

expectation of many who had come to witness the opening ceremony, and one of the visitors relieved himself by composing the following verse:—

> "Boston, Boston, Boston!
> Thou hast naught to boast on,
> But a Grand Sluice, and a high steeple;
> A proud conceited ignorant people,
> And a coast where souls are lost on."

The General Commissioners expended in the erection of the sluice and other drainage works the sum of £58,650, which was raised on mortgage; and for the defraying of which, and for current expenses, they were authorized to collect taxes not exceeding one shilling per acre on the first, second, third, and fourth districts, and sixpence per acre on the fifth and sixth. Half-year lands were to pay only two-thirds of these amounts; and common lands one-half so long as they remained in that condition, but as soon as they became improved lands they were to be subject to the full rate. The Commissioners were further empowered to enclose common lands to the extent of 800 acres in the West, 600 acres in the Wildmore, and 1000 acres in Holland Fens, and to let the same on lease for 21 years, the rents being applied to the purposes of drainage.

These works having been successfully carried out as designed by the promoters, proved of immediate advantage to the drainage of the fens bordering on the Witham, between Lincoln and Chapel-hill; but the East and West Fens still remained in a drowned state. A separate chapter will be devoted to the history of their reclamation. The waters of Holland Fen and of the districts adjoining were subsequently provided for by the drainage carried out by the Black Sluice Commissioners.

The river was made navigable for barges and small craft as far as Lincoln, and it might have been thought that, having carried their scheme out to its completion, the General Commissioners would for the future simply have the duty of maintaining the works in good order, and that the drainage of the level would remain in a perfect condition; but within a very few years it became only too apparent that the warning which the Commissioners received at the time was too well founded, and that by obstructing the free passage of the tides, by the erection of the Grand Sluice across the river, a very serious error had been committed. For a short time the collecting the waters together and speedily discharging them through the remodelled drains into the Witham, and through the new cut into the haven, had a beneficial effect in scouring out its bed and lowering the level of the water throughout the fens; but very soon the consequences which invariably follow the erection of weirs or dams of any description across a tidal river became apparent. The tidal stream, arrested in its progress by the sluice, became quiescent, and the silt and mud brought up and held in suspension, so long as the water was in motion, sunk by its own gravity directly stagnation took place, and gradually formed a deposit on the bed of the haven. Previous to the year 1800, in average winter seasons, the water never fell below nine feet six inches on the cill, and in floods rose considerably higher; while in summer time, there not being back water sufficient to remove the deposit, it accumulated to such a degree as completely to close the doors. *(Chapman's Facts and Remarks.)* A few years after the erection of the sluice, it appears, from old records, to have risen to a height of ten feet on the cill, completely stopping all communication between the barges navigating the Witham and the vessels employed in exporting and importing coals and other commodities. The drainage also became defective. The most perfect system of interior drainage is useless unless it has a good outfall or discharge for its water. The outfall of the Witham being blocked up in summer, and being so much higher than formerly in winter, the low lands could not get rid of their waters by natural means, but had to resort to pumping, the power being supplied by windmills in the first instance, followed in later years by steam engines. All the low-lying districts on the Witham provided themselves with engines before or in the beginning of the present century; and these have continued to work up to the present time, at a very considerable annual cost in coals, attendance, and repairs. The present power of the engines engaged in pumping the water which drains into the Witham above the Grand Sluice is not less than an aggregate of three hundred and fifty horse-power.

In certain situations, there is no doubt that sluices are necessary and highly advantageous. In fact they are absolutely required at the end of a canal or artificial cut discharging into a tidal stream carrying deposit of any kind in its waters, where such a cut has no natural stream or back water. In such a case, if the tides are allowed a free course, a small quantity of deposit is left at the extreme point touched by the spring tides, which, unless washed away in course of a reasonable time by fresh water coming from lands above, gradually accumulates and extends lower and lower down the stream. In exact ratio as this process goes on, the scouring effect of the tides lessens, until at last the bed of the channel becomes dry land. To guard against this then it is necessary to erect at the point where the canal joins the tidal stream a sluice to prevent the ingress of the tides; but it is also equally necessary that this sluice should be placed so as to discharge into a stream having a free current of water continually passing through it, sufficient to prevent the deposit contained in its water from settling and raising its bed. Such a main artery should the Witham be, and would be were it not for the obstruction to the tidal stream caused by the Grand Sluice, which has not only injured it as the outfall for the several sluices discharging their contents into it, and for the lands draining immediately by it, but also for the navigation of the port of Boston. There is no doubt that if the tides had free course up the river, and ran through the town of Boston from three to four hours, as they did before the erection of the Grand Sluice, the strength of the returning ebbs would keep the bed of the river scoured out to its natural level; and consequently lower the water on the cills of all the sluices throughout the level, allowing the lands to drain by gravitation, and rendering unnecessary the use of steam power.

The amount of water brought down from the high lands by the Witham throughout a course of nearly forty miles, and by its tributaries, is amply sufficient to remove the small deposit left at the head of the high spring tides, the only place where this would occur. It may be said, if the tides are sufficient to keep the river scoured out and deepened, how is it to be accounted for that the river was in the lost condition that it was before the erection of the sluice in 1751. The answer is obvious. The management of the river had been so completely neglected that its channel was full of weeds and obstructions of all kinds; the water was not confined within the regular channels; nor was the size of these channels efficiently regulated. Numerous breaches in the banks allowed the stream to wander over the fens, and so it became scattered and its power weakened; till ultimately, instead of scouring and deepening, it fed and added to the other obstructions in the river. Neither were any steps taken to counteract the effect on the outfall of the river caused by the silting up of the Estuary, a process which has been for ages and is now slowly but steadily going on, and which even at this time demands the serious attention of those interested in the efficiency of the Witham as the outfall for their drainage.*

---

* More detailed information on this subject is given in the author's pamphlet on the "Outfall of the River Witham."

In the year 1802 Mr. Rennie was requested by the General Commissioners for Drainage and Navigation to report to them on the state of the Witham, with a view to suggest some improvement. As no result followed this report it will only be necessary to say that among several minor works it recommended the erection of an additional sluice, and making a new cut from the Witham to Skirbeck Quarter. In the year 1807 Mr. Rennie made another report as to the state of the Witham, and suggested several improvements, including its deepening, so as to make the bed of the river from Boston to Washingborough on a level with the cill of the Grand Sluice, allowing the pen height of the water there to be reduced without stopping the navigation, and the erection of a new lock and sluices at the latter place; also a new cut from Horsley Deeps to the parish of Fiskerton.

In April, 1807, at a meeting of the Commissioners, a series of resolutions were passed stating that whereas by the enclosure of the West and Wildmore Fens their funds had been considerably increased, they proposed to improve the navigation of the Witham on the plan proposed by Mr. Rennie; and that it was desirable that its management should be handed over to a company, if one could be formed for this purpose. In the following year an Act was obtained for effecting this and carrying out these works of improvement, which recited that the powers granted by the Act of 1791 were not sufficient to enable the Commissioners to execute all the works therein contemplated, and that several of them were then uncompleted; that in consequence much land was liable to injury from floods, and the commerce of the country greatly interrupted. It will be unnecessary to refer further to this, as the money authorized (£70,000) was never raised, and the Act was entirely repealed by a subsequent one.

In the year 1811 Mr. Rennie was again called to advise the Commissioners, and he proposed an amended scheme on that of

1807 for the improvement of the river. It had long since been admitted that the drainage and navigation interfered with each other, and the object the Commissioners had in view was to make provision for the carrying out of the two trusts in the way most beneficial to each, and so that the one should not injure the other. Mr. Rennie's report and recommendation having been adopted, an Act was obtained in the following session (52, Geo. III., cap. 108) by which the powers vested in the Commissioners of Navigation by the former Act were transferred to a Company of Proprietors, who were to undertake the whole management of the navigation and the works pertaining thereto. The tolls were fixed at three shillings per ton on all goods conveyed between Lincoln and Boston, or for shorter distances three halfpence per ton per mile. The duties of the proprietors of the navigation, and of the Drainage Commissioners, as to the maintenance of the different portions of the river and its embankments were set out, and the following new works, as recommended by Mr. Rennie, authorized: —The scouring out, widening and deepening, and embanking the Witham, from the Grand Sluice to Lincoln, the lower end to be finished to a fifty feet bottom, diminishing to a thirty-six feet at Horsley Deeps: whence a new cut, with a thirty feet bottom, was to be made at Washingborough; a new lock was to be made at the entrance of the new cut at Horsley Deeps, with a rise of three feet, and another at Stamp-end, in Lincoln, with a rise of four feet. The cill of the former was to be level with the bed of the river, which at this point was to be six feet under the gauge mark of the Grand Sluice. The old locks across the river at Barlings and Kirkstead, and Stamp-end, were to be removed.

In order to provide for the flood waters from the west side of Lincoln, a weir twenty-eight feet in width was to be made in the east bank of the Witham, at the head of Bargate-drain, which, together with the Sincil dyke, was to be scoured out and deepened, and a new cut made from the junction of the latter with the Witham, along the back of its south bank to Horsley Deeps, to join the river below the new lock; and a dolph or soak dyke cut parallel with the north bank of the river from Barlings Eau, as far upwards as should be found necessary to take the water lying on the north side of the navigation.

To carry out these works, the Company of Proprietors were authorized to raise amongst themselves a sum of £120,000 in shares of £100, and to borrow, on the mortgage of the tolls and dues, the sum of £60,000. In consideration of the benefit to the drainage by the improvement of the river, and an agreement on the part of the Navigation Proprietors to advance and apply the sum of £30,000 towards the execution of drainage works, the Commissioners were to contribute the sum of £1400 per annum out of their general funds; and a like sum of £1400 out of the funds specially provided by this Act to the Company of Proprietors. To enable them to do this they were authorized to collect additional taxes on the first and third districts of one shilling and sixpence,— one shilling, and sixpence per acre respectively, according to benefit received,—and of threepence per acre on the fifth district.

In carrying out these works several antiquities were discovered. In making the excavation for the Horsley Deeps Lock a canoe was found eight feet under the surface. It had been hollowed out of an oak tree, was thirty feet eight inches long, and measured three feet in the widest part. Other canoes were also dug up, one of which is deposited amongst the collection of antiquities in the British Museum.

In connection with the navigation of the Witham, communication was effected with the towns of Sleaford and Horncastle by navigable canals, which were constructed under Acts granted in the 32nd year of George the Third's reign,—the former by the widening and improving the Kyme Eau, which, from very early times, had been in a navigable condition, as before referred to; and the latter by making a new cut to Tattershall, and extending the same into the Bane and rendering that river navigable as far as Horncastle. By means of the Fossdyke, an ancient canal first made by the Romans, and subsequently cleaned out and deepened by Henry the First, the Witham was connected with the Trent and the vast system of water communication extending nearly all over England.

These works of improvement in the Witham did not meet with the general approval of the districts concerned in the drainage. The proprietors of lands on the west side of the Witham employed Mr. W. Chapman to advise them, and in a report dated Newcastle, January 14, 1808, he states his most decided opinion that no improvement could be expected until the Grand Sluice was removed and the outfall improved by straightening and confining the channel to deep water. These remarks appear to be well founded, and the works as carried out to have been of more advantage to the navigation than the drainage; for not long afterwards the fens adjoining the river found it necessary to employ steam power to supplant their old windmills, which were deemed not equal to the duty of pumping off the water with sufficient rapidity and regularity. In order to prevent this expenditure, Mr. Rennie was instructed by the General Commissioners to report as to the best means of improving the outfall and lowering the water in the Witham sufficiently to allow of the drainage of the lowest lands by gravitation; and further as to the effect on the general interests of the trusts by the proposed pumping schemes.

Mr. Rennie, in two reports made in the year 1830, dated respectively the 9th of August and the 17th September, admits that the state of drainage in the first district was very imperfect, and that the chief impediments to the discharge of the waters arose from two causes—the first the obstructed state of the outfall of Boston Haven, between the Grand Sluice and Hobhole; and the second to the Grand Sluice and the inadequacy of the interior drains to convey the downfall waters into the Witham. With respect to the first, he refers to the improvements already carried out by the Corporation of Boston, by straightening the river and making the new cut through Burton's Marsh, and by the removal of the old wooden bridge with its piers, and the erection in its place of the present iron structure; but he thought that the outfall was capable of very considerable further improvement, and proposed a plan, the particulars of which will be treated of more fully in a succeeding chapter, and he also recommended the making of a new cut through the Marshes from the Black Sluice to Bell's Reach, at a cost of £89,313.

For a removal of the second cause of impediment from the confined state of the outlet of the river, and the water constantly obliged to be held up for the purposes of navigation, he proposed that a new sluice should be erected between the Grand Sluice and the iron bridge; from this a new cut should be made, in a direct line, to join the North Forty Foot, which was to be deepened and cleaned out to the Sleaford navigation, and from there the present line of the Hales Head Dyke should be enlarged and deepened as far as Washingborough, the estimated cost being £52,873.

It is hardly necessary to say that these recommendations were not carried out, but the Commissioners, at a meeting held in 1832, passed several resolutions stating that it was their opinion that the steam engines proposed to be erected by the first and third districts would prove injurious to the banks of the river and the drainage of the other districts, and therefore they determined to oppose the powers sought to be obtained from Parliament by those parties.

The next event in the history of the Witham was the construction of the Great Northern Railway along its banks, and the iron road succeeded the river as the great highway from Boston to

Lincoln. The rights of the proprietors were transferred to the the Great Northern Railway Company by their Act of 1846, and they now hold the navigation in their own hands, and have assumed the liabilities of the original owners. These liabilities have since been a matter of considerable litigation. In the spring of 1862, owing to an unusually heavy rainfall, the river Witham became flooded above its ordinary height, and on the 28th March the bank of the South Delph gave way, the water pouring through the breach and inundating a large tract of land in Branston Fen. An action was brought against the Great Northern Railway Company for compensation, the case (Cawdron *v.* Great Northern Railway Company) being tried at the following Lincoln Summer Assizes, and a verdict given for the plaintiff. A rule *nisi* was obtained to set aside this verdict, on the ground that the judge at the trial had not allowed the question to go to the jury as to whether the mischief had not been caused by default of the Witham Drainage Commissioners in not providing a proper outlet for the waters in the river below Horsley Deeps, which had consequently backed up into the South Delph, and so caused the flooding. The rule was subsequently discharged by the Court of Exchequer, July 6th, 1863, Baron Bramwell remarking, "I desire not to have it supposed that I discharge the rule because I am of opinion that the Great Northern Railway Company would have been liable if the banks were broken through the water being pent back upon them improperly by persons below; but the rule is discharged upon the ground that we cannot collect from the summing up of the learned judge that he took a different view on the trial." *(Law Times Reports.)* The state of these banks and of the river, the water in which at its upper end in heavy floods is often nearly on a level with their top, has been a source of anxiety to the General Commissioners.

On the 19th of March, 1861, a deputation from the commission waited on Mr. Hawkshaw, C.E., in London, to consult that gentleman with reference to the state of the drainage, the immediate object being the improvement of the condition of the east and west Fens, but Mr. Hawkshaw was also directed to turn his attention to a scheme for the general improvement of all the fens under the jurisdiction of the Witham Trust. The general scheme recommended by Mr. Hawkshaw was the old plan so often urged on the attention of the Commissioners, namely, the improvement of the outfall of the river by straightening the haven, and conducting the water in a confined channel to the sea, and so lowering the water throughout the whole level; a fuller account of which will be given in a subsequent chapter. But insuperable difficulties seem ever to have opposed themselves to a general scheme of this kind, and the Commissioners had to fall back on such measures as they could carry out themselves without the assistance of other trusts. Mr. Hawkshaw was therefore directed " to examine and report on the state of the drainage of the river Witham above the Grand Sluice, embracing the 1st, 3rd, and 5th districts, with a view to any improvement that could be effected." Mr. Hawkshaw accordingly, in the autumn of 1862, caused a survey to be made of the river from the Grand Sluice to Lincoln. With the data thus obtained, and from facts gathered from other sources, he drew up his report, and laid before the Commissioners the works that he considered necessary for putting the upper part of the river in as efficient a state as possible under its present condition in connection with the navigation, the existence of the Grand Sluice, and the state of Boston Haven; which, when completed, would enable the Commissioners to lower the height of the water in the channel, and so improve the drainage of the lands, without hindering the navigation; and by strengthening the banks, remove all cause of apprehension as to their safety. The estimated cost of the works was £53,000, the advantage to be gained by the drainage,—lowering the level of the water in the Witham an average of two feet.

The Commissioners hesitated some time before adopting this scheme of interior improvement, but at last, finding that no general plan was likely to be successfully carried out, three years afterwards they obtained an Act "for the further improvement of the drainage and navigation by the River Witham," which received the Royal Assent on the 19th of June, 1865. Under the powers of this Act the Commissioners were authorised to execute the following works :—To deepen and scour out the river Witham, from a point about six miles above Boston to Horsley Deeps, so that the bottom should throughout this length be on a dead level; to deepen and scour and strengthen the banks of the Old Witham, Barling Eau, Billinghay Skirth, and the several tributaries in connection with them; to alter and lower the cills of the several sluices of the above streams, and also those of the Sleaford and Horncastle navigation, and the cills of the several delphs belonging to the parishes of Timberland, Metheringham, Stixwould, Dunston, Branston, and Washingborough.

The Great Northern Railway Company, as the owners of the navigation, were authorised to scour out and deepen and strengthen the banks of the south Delph, and to lower the cill of Anton's Gowt and Horsley Deeps Locks, and re-build the latter, if necessary; and for this purpose they were empowered to raise the sum of £10,000 by the creation of new capital to that extent. The General Commissioners were authorised to borrow a sum not exceeding £55,000 on mortgage of new taxes, to be levied for the purposes of this Act, the extinction of the debt being provided for by the re-payment of thirty-five annual instalments. The lands in the first, third, and fifth districts are taxed for these special works in four classes, as arranged by the Act of 1812, with an additional annual payment of three shillings, two shillings and sixpence, two shillings, and one shilling per acre respectively.

Another very necessary and important power was given to the Commissioners, namely, that of making bye-laws for the regulation of the fishery, and other incidental rights and privileges attaching to the river and the drainage. It has been already mentioned that the Witham was, in olden times, renowned for the quantity and quality of its fish; and if its fishery were now placed under proper jurisdiction there is no doubt it would once again become a valuable property: but the general licence that has hitherto been accorded to poachers of all kinds, both to use and abuse the right of fishing, has almost totally destroyed the river as a means either of profitable production or recreation. The Commissioners now have power to make bye-laws, and appoint bailiffs to see that their orders are carried out; and these once made and promulgated, offenders against the rules will be liable to penalties. As the carrying out of stringent rules will be for the general benefit of all in any way interested in the pisciculture of the land, and of this district in particular, it is to be hoped that the Commissioners will feel the desirability of making and publishing bye-laws.

There now only remains a mention of the fact that the works authorised to be executed by the last Act are at this time being carried out by Mr. Hoborrow, who has taken the contract, and who is at this time engaged in deepening the river by means of steam dredgers, the material excavated being deposited on the banks by a mud elevator specially invented and constructed by the contractor for this work.

CHAPTER III.

THE EAST, WEST, AND WILDMORE FENS.

These fens form the Fourth District of the Witham Commission, and the account of their reclamation belongs properly to the last chapter; but it is considered that their history is of sufficient importance to deserve a separate notice.

The East Fen was the last to be enclosed in this district, and the recollection of many persons now living dates back to the time when " it afforded little benefit to the realm other than fish and fowl, with overmuch harbour to a rude and almost barbarous sort of lazy and beggarly people." The state of the fens before their reclamation has been described as presenting in the winter season, in some parts, the appearance of a chain of lakes, bordered by a thick crop of reeds; and in others, of one vast sheet of water, with mounds or islets dotted here and there, on which the few and scattered inhabitants erected their huts; and whose only way of access to one another, and of communication with the towns or villages near, was by means of small boats or canoes, which they paddled along with a pole, and also used in their fishing and fowling expeditions. Living thus isolated and apart from all the comforts and advantages of civilized life, deprived of the humanising effect of churches and religious instruction, and the kind care and soothing influence of a pastor, these people were in little better condition than the aborigines of New Zealand or Australia. Macaulay speaks of them as a half savage people, leading an amphibious life, sometimes rowing, sometimes wading from one firm mound to another, and known as " Breedlings," a name which had succeeded the ancient "Girvii," and afterwards given place to that of "Fen Slodgers," by which appellation they were known up to the beginning of the present century.*

These men were violently opposed to any attempts to alter the state of the fens, believing they had a kind of vested interest in the fishing and fowling, by which they gained their scanty subsistence. Although their condition was very miserable, they nevertheless enjoyed a sort of wild liberty amidst the watery wastes, which they were not disposed to give up. Though they might alternately burn and shiver with ague, and become prematurely bowed and twisted with rheumatism, still the fens were their native land, such as it was, and their only source of subsistence, precarious though it might be. The fens were their commons on which their geese grazed. They furnished them with food, though the finding thereof was full of adventure and hazard. What cared the fenmen for the drowning of the land? Did not the water bring them fish, and the fish attract wild fowl, which they could snare and shoot? Thus the proposal to drain the fens and convert them into wholesome and fruitful lands, however important in a national point of view, as enlarging the resources and increasing the wealth of the country, had no attraction whatever in the eyes of the "slodgers." They muttered their discontent, and everywhere met the reclaimers with opposition, and frequently assembled to fill up the cuts which the labourers had dug, and to pull down the banks which they had constructed; and to such an extent was this carried that in some places the men had frequently to work under the protection of an armed guard. But their numbers were too few, and they were too widely

---

* The engraving at the end of this chapter is taken by permission from Mr. Thompson's History of Boston, to whom it was given "by a friend whose memory reached back nearly three quarters of a century. It represents the costume and appearance of two of the *Slodgers* returning from a fowling excursion, and the general appearance of the East Fen at that time."

scattered, to make any combined effort at resistance. (*Smiles' Lives of the Engineers.*) In addition to the opposition of the natives, other agencies were brought to bear against the fen drainers. Satirical poems and ballads were composed and sung with great applause in the fen towns, and their cause was even advocated by men of learning and social standing. Amongst others, Fuller in his history speaks of the attempted enclosure of the fens as a trespass on the divine prerogative for man to presume to give other bounds to the water than that which God had appointed; and he intimates that Providence had specially left this district for the production of fish and fowl, and of sedge, turf, and reeds.

In winter time the fens were almost entirely covered with water, poured on to them from the high lands, by which they were bordered; but in summer, when this had drained away and evaporated, the greater part of the land became covered with a coarse kind of grass, and afforded a feeding ground to the cattle of the farmers residing in the surrounding parishes, all of which had a right of common in these fens.

So early as the reign of Edward VI. a code of fen laws had been enacted for defining the rights and privileges of the commoners, and for the prevention of disputes and robbery. The first code, drawn up by the great inquest of the soke of Bolingbroke, held in 1548, was several times renewed, and together with additional laws, passed in Queen Elizabeth's reign, remained in force until the enclosure of the fens at the beginning of the present century. The code consisted of seventy-two articles, a short summary of which may be interesting, as affording an insight into a state of society now passed away for ever. One of the first rules related to the brands or marks which each person stocking the fens was required to place upon his cattle. Each parish had a separate mark, and no man was allowed to turn cattle out to common until they were marked with the town brand. No foreigner or person not having common right was allowed to fish or fowl at any time, or gather any tu bary or fodder in the East Fen, without a licence from the approver, under a penalty of twenty shillings for each offence ; a like penalty was also attached to the following offences :—Putting diseased cattle on the fens ; disturbing the cattle by baiting with savage dogs ; for leaving any dead animal unburied for more than three days ; for putting swine on the fen unrung, or geese which were not pinioned and foot-marked ; for taking or leaving dogs there after sunset ; for bringing up crane birds out of the East Fen. No person was allowed to gather wool who was not above twelve years of age, except impotent persons ; no cattle were to be driven out of the fens except between sunrise and sunset ; all cattle were to be " roided " out of the East Fen before St. Barnaby's day yearly ; no reed thatch, reed star, or bolt was to be mown before it was two years' growth ; each sheaf of thatch gathered or bound up was to be a yard in compass ; wythes were only to be cut between Michaelmas and May-day.

By a law, passed in Queen Elizabeth's reign, every township in the parts of Holland, claiming common in the West Fen, was ordered to show to the Queen's steward, at the next court-day, its charter or title to such common right. No swan, crane, or bittern eggs, or any eggs excepting those of ducks and geese, were allowed to be brought out of the fens. No fodder was to be mown in the East or West Fen before Midsummer-day annually. No person was allowed to use any sort of net or other engines to take or kill any fowl, commonly called moulted ducks, in any of the fens before Midsummer-day yearly. *(Thompson's History of Boston.)* A code of seventeen articles was also devised by the fishermen's jury, relative to the fish and fishing in the fens. The principal fish referred to were pike, eels, roach, and perch.

Camden, whose description of England was written before the enclosure of the fens, gives a quaint account of the feathered tribes frequenting these parts. The narrative says: " that at certain seasons of the year, not to mention fish, amazing flights of fowl are found all over this part of the country, not the common ones which were in great esteem in other places, such as teal, quails, woodcocks, pheasants, partridges, &c., but such as have no Latin names, the delicacies of tables and the food of heroes, fit for the palates of the great—puittes, godwittes, knots, which I take to mean Canute's birds, for they are supposed to come hither from Denmark; dotterells, so called from their extravagant dotishness, which occasions these imitative birds to be caught by candle-light. If he only puts out his arm they put out a wing, and if his leg they do the same; in short, whatever the fowler does the bird does the same, till the net is drawn over it." Macaulay adds to this description by telling us that the marshes of Lincolnshire were covered during some months of every year by immense clouds of cranes. Nor must the mention of the fen nightingales or frogs be omitted, for they are said to have especially abounded.

The Fens have long been celebrated for the large flocks of geese kept by the inhabitants, which were bred as much for the sake of their feathers as for food. The practice was to pluck the small feathers from these birds five times a year, and the larger feathers and quills twice. This plan of taking the feathers from the geese when alive was not so cruel as at first sight it would seem to be, it being alleged that at the exact time when they were taken they were quite loose and separated easily, without pain, from the skin; and the practice was justified from the fact that live quills were far superior to those taken from the birds when dead. Arthur Young in his survey of Lincolnshire gives the value " of the feathers of a dead goose as worth six-pence, three giving a pound ; but plucking alive does not yield more than three pence a head per annum. Some wing them every quarter. Taking the feathers from each goose, which will sell at five shillings per thousand, plucked geese pay in feathers one shilling a head in Wildmore Fen." The feathers of geese were considered superior to any others for stuffing beds, and large quantities are now imported from abroad to meet the demand which the Lincolnshire fens used to supply, and the quill has long since been almost superseded by the steel pen. Some proprietors used to have flocks of from one to two thousand geese, exclusive of goslings. During the breeding season the birds were lodged in the same house with the inhabitants, and even in their very bed chambers. Three rows of coarse wicker pens, placed one above the other, were fitted up in the houses ; each bird had its separate nest, which it kept possession of during the time of sitting. A gozzard, or gooseherd, used to attend to the flock, and twice a day drove the whole flock to the water, and would assist those that sat in the upper stories to their nests without misplacing a single bird. *(Gough's and Camden's Brittania.)*

A notice of the ' decoys,' or receptacles for catching wild fowl, must not be omitted from this description of the peculiar institutions of these fens.

Decoys were formerly very numerous and very profitable. Ten decoys in the West Fen, it is stated, during one winter furnished the enormous number of 31,200 birds. At the time of the original drainage of the Bedford Level, under the "Lynn law," the pools of the decoys, or "meeres," were specially excepted from the grants made to the undertakers, and they were restricted from draining them ; but the wild fowl has since had to yield to the drainer, and the site of the greater part of these inland lakes is now only indicated by their name—the mere having become dry land. A few still remain, the only one in this neighbourhood being at Friskney, from which large quantities of birds are still supplied to the markets of Boston and other places. A decoy is formed by pools surrounded by trees and plantations, and branching off from them are small channels or ditches called "pipes." At the time of catching the birds, these pipes are covered over with nets, which rest on hoops, and are terminated by a drawing net. Into these the wild fowl are enticed by various devices; but the usual mode is by means of a decoy duck, trained for the purpose. This bird is taught to obey the whistle of the decoy man, who tempts it to swim up the trapping tunnel when he sees a number of wild fowl; these following the tame one, and being led into the channel, are then enclosed and ultimately taken by the net. These decoy birds will fly away to sea in the morning, where meeting and consorting with strange birds during the daytime, at night they will lead them away inland to the decoy ponds. Dogs are also kept, who by their sagacity and training are of the greatest assistance to the keeper in drawing the birds into the nets. Of such importance were decoys deemed, that special acts of the legislature have been passed for their regulation and protection. By an act passed in Queen Anne's reign, the clauses of which were re-enacted in the 10th year of George II., it was made an offence against the law to take birds at unseasonable times, under a penalty of five shillings for every bird. Mallards, teal, and widgeon are the birds principally taken, and a good decoy is still a very lucrative concern.

The prophecies of the decay which would fall upon the country if the race of fen-men were deprived of their valuable pools for pike, fish, and wild fowl, have long since been exploded. The population has grown in numbers, in health, and in comfort, with the progress of drainage and reclamation. The fens are no longer the lurking places of disease, but are as salubrious as any other part of England; dreary swamps are supplanted by pleasant pastures, and the haunts of pike and wild fowl have become the habitations of industrious farmers and husbandmen. But this result has only been arrived at by a vast amount of skill and labour, and the expenditure of large sums of money. It is the history of the various attempts which have been made to reclaim the East, West, and Wildmore Fens that will occupy the remainder of this chapter.

The early history of the West and Wildmore Fens is included in that of the Witham; such drainage as it had was provided under the direction of the Court of Sewers, by means of Anton's Gowt, and another small sluice at Maud Foster, which was the outlet to a natural sewer or drain which ran from Cowbridge to the Scire-beck, near Podder's or Peter's Bridge, before Maud Foster drain was cut in 1631. The East Fen, being much lower and further removed from the high lands, and the religious establishments on the Witham, remained untouched till a much later period.

In Queen Elizabeth's reign some idea was entertained of making an attempt for the recovery of the East Fen, and a survey was made by order of the Queen, from which it was estimated to contain 5000 acres or thereabouts; and it was considered half of this, being the skirts, hills, and outrings could conveniently be drained; but the other half, consisting of deep holes and pits, could not be recovered. Beyond the survey nothing further seems to have been attempted until the next reign, when, shortly after James the First's accession to the throne, a series of destructive floods burst the embankments of the fens on the east coast, and swept over farms, homesteads, and villages, drowning large numbers of people and cattle. The King, on being informed of the great calamity which had befallen the inhabitants of the fens, principally through the decay of the old works of drainage and embankment, declared that, for the honour of his kingdom, he would not any longer suffer these countries to be abandoned to the will of the waters, nor to let them lie waste and unprofitable; and that if no one else would undertake their drainage, he himself would become the "undertaker." But a measure of taxation for the recovery of these lands, which was accordingly proposed to the Commons, was rejected, and the King, restricted in his means, confined his attention to works on the Great Level of Cambridgeshire.

In the sixth year of King Charles the First, a Court of Sewers was held at Boston, and Commissioners, specially appointed by the King, sat there to make enquiry into the state of this district. After hearing evidence on the subject, they recited that the whole of the fens, from the Witham to the coast, were drowned and surrounded lands most part of the year, and that these lands were capable of recovery, and they therefore decreed that a tax of ten shillings per acre should be levied for the repairs of the natural outfalls at Waynflete Haven, Black Gote, Symon Gote, Maud Foster Gote, New Gote, and Anton Gote, as also any other cuts or drains that should be found necessary to be made or enlarged. In default of payment of the tax, a bargain was to be made with Sir Anthony Thomas, who proposed to become the undertaker for the drainage for a certain quantity of the drowned land which was to become his property on his successfully completing the work. The tax not being paid, the fens were handed over to the undertakers, who, in September, 1631, commenced their works and made a New Cut or " great and navigable stream, three miles in length, from Cowbridge to the Haven, near Boston, and at the end of it the old Maud Foster Gowt was replaced by ' a very large gowt of stone and timber.' " They also made many other petty sewers, gutters, and streams, having their courses to the said main river, and over them were erected many bridges and other works, done with so much diligence that three years after the commencement, a decree was made by the Court of Sewers " that, on a view of the late surrounded grounds, viz., East and West Fens, North Fen, Earles Fen, Armetro Fen, and Wildmore Fen, and other the drowned commons and adjacent surrounded grounds, lying on the north and north east of the river Witham, within the extent of the said commission, they adjudged the same to be so drained as that they were fit for arable, meadow, and pasture. And that out of three thousand acres of pits, deeps, and holes which formerly existed, there now only remained sixteen hundred and seventy-three acres." And they confirmed to Sir Anthony Thomas a grant of one-half of the commons land in the East Fen, and a third of the severals adjacent thereto; and also one-fourth of the West Fen and the surrounded grounds adjoining. Two thousand five hundred acres of the lands so granted were made liable to the maintenance of the works, and the rents were to be paid into the hands of the Mayor of Boston, to be employed for and about the repairs of the bridges, gates, and drains, until they amounted to the sum of two thousand pounds, to the extent of which amount they were always answerable. (*Dugdale.*) The total quantity acquired by the adventurers, as recompense for their undertaking, was altogether 16,300 acres, which brought them a rental of £8000 a year. The amount expended in the drainage and reclamation was £30,000, and they subsequently spent £20,000 in improving their lands and in constructing buildings.

For seven years they enjoyed their occupation, building houses, sowing corn, and feeding cattle thereon; at the end of that time the commoners, " finding that done, of which they themselves despaired, made several clamours, but finding no relief in time of peace, they resolved to try if force and violence would compass that, which neither justice nor reason could give; and to that end, a little before Edgehill fight, in 1642, they being incensed by some then in faction, took arms, and in a riotous manner they fell upon the adventurers, broke the sluices, laid waste their lands, threw in their fences, spoiled their corn, demolished their houses, and forcibly retained possession of the land."

The Adventurers, finding that the Sheriff and other local authorities could not afford them protection, petitioned the Houses of Lords and Commons. With the former they were successful, but being opposed by the Commoners failed to obtain an Act from the latter. The Commoners stated in their petition that Sir A. Thomas had not fairly obtained the decree from the Court of Sewers in the first instance; that he had not fulfilled his bargain, as the lands—particularly in the West and Wildmore Fens—were not improved by his works; further that the quantity of land granted to him was excessive; and that he was already well paid for what he had done by his seven years' possession. Having heard both parties, the House of Commons ordered that the Sheriff and Justices of the Peace should prevent and suppress riots, if any should happen, but expressly declared that they did not intend thereby to prejudice the parties interested in point of title to the lands, or to hinder the commoners in the legal pursuit of their interest. Upon this the parties commenced proceedings at common law against the Adventurers, in which they were successful.

For about one hundred and fifty years these fens continued to be very imperfectly drained by the sewers and sluices provided by Sir Anthony Thomas, and their state during this period, as shown by the following description, proves that his scheme was very deficient, and that the Commoners were justified in the statements they made before the Houses of Parliament:—" The fen called the West Fen is the place where the ruffs and reeves resort in greatest numbers, and many other sorts of water fowl which do not require the shelter of reeds and rushes migrate hither to breed, for this fen is bare, having been imperfectly drained by narrow canals which intersect it for many miles. Twenty parishes in the Soke of Bolingbroke have right of common on it, but an enclosure is now in agitation. The East Fen is quite in a state of nature, and exhibits a specimen of what the country was before the introduction of draining. It is a vast tract of morass, intermixed with numbers of lakes, from half a mile to two or three miles in circuit, communicating with each other by narrow reedy straits. They are very shallow, none above four or five feet deep, but abound with pike, perch, ruffs, bream, tench, dace, eels, &c. The reeds which cover the fens are cut annually for thatching not only cottages, but many very good houses. The multitudes of stares that roost in these weeds in winter break down many by perching on them. A stock of reeds well harvested and stacked is worth two or three hundred pounds. The birds which inhabit the different Fens are very numerous. Besides the common wild duck, wild geese, garganies, pochards, shovellers, and teals breed here, pewit, gulls, and black terns abound : a few of the great terns or tickets are seen among them. The great crested grebes, called gaunts, are found in the East Fen. The lesser crested, the black and dusky, and the little grebe, cootes, water-hens, and spotted water-hens, water-rails, ruffs, red-shanks, lapwings or wypes, red-breasted godwits, and whimbrels are inhabitants of these fens. The godwits breed near Washingborough, three miles east of Lincoln ; the whimbrels only appear for a fortnight in May and then quit the country." *(Camden.)* The reeds referred to in the above description grew in great numbers in the fens before the drainage and reclamation. They are described as having had the appearance, when growing, of extensive fields of wheat. In the latter part of the summer they were cut down and reaped like corn, and afterwards carefully dried and dressed, and being tied in bundles or sheaves were sold for thatching houses. Great numbers of houses and barns, and even the churches bordering on the Fens of Norfolk, were covered with this thatch. It made a neat and endurable cover, and lasted for thirty or forty years.

In the year 1800 Mr. Rennie was directed by the Witham Commissioners to report on the drainage of the East, West, and Wildmore Fens, and after a survey made he delivered his report, bearing date April 7th, a second report being presented on the 1st of September.

From these it appears that the drainage of the Wildmore and part of the West Fen was made through Anton's Gowt, by means of the sluice erected by the Witham Commissioners at the time the river was straightened, as detailed in the preceding chapter, the cill of which was two feet above the cill of the Grand Sluice. Through this sluice also were discharged the waters from the high country lying in the lordships of Kirkby, Revesby, Mareham, Tumby, and Coningsby, but in times of flood the Witham over-rode the waters from these parts, and they were driven back through Medlam Drain and West House Skye to Cherry Corner, whence it found its way by Mill-drain or Stone Bridge-drain to Maud Foster's Gowt, which consisted of a single opening, 13 feet wide, its cill being three inches lower than the cill of the Grand Sluice. Low water of spring tides at that time stood about four feet nine inches on the cill, and the general surface of the lands in the West and Wildmore Fens was nine feet above the cill, allowing a fall of four feet three inches from the surface to low water mark. The lowest d in the Fen, called "No Man's Friend," was one foot be   rest, and in the autumn of 1799 was covered with water   depth. The total quantity of land in Wildmore Fen was   es of high lands, and 7714 acres of Fen lands; in the   5473 high lands, and 11,451 of Fen lands: a total   acres.

The East Fen and East Holland towns were very imperfectly drained by Maud Foster's Gowt. Fishtoft and Butterwick had separate sluices, under the control of the Court of Sewers; and part of the water of Friskney was raised by a water engine, and sent to sea by a small gowt. The general surface of the East Fen and of Wrangle Common was found to be about eight feet above the cill of the old Maud Foster Sluice. The East Fen was computed to contain 12,424 acres, and the East Holland towns 26,000 acres.

The scheme recommended by Mr. Rennie, and adopted by the Commissioners, will be more fully detailed hereafter. A very strong feeling prevailed that the whole of the drainage of the East Fen should be discharged into the river at the old outlet at Maud Foster, on the principle that for the preservation of an outfall the tributary stream should be conducted to its channel at the highest point possible. Others more intimately connected with the district contended that the main object to be sought was the efficient drainage of the fens, irrespective of other considerations, and therefore advocated a new cut to Wainfleet Haven; while a third plan was that which was finally adopted, being a compromise between the two, by which the water was to be conveyed by a new cut through the centre of the East Fen, discharging into the river near Fishtoft Gowt.

Mr. Rennie dismissed the Wainfleet Haven Scheme as incompatible with a thorough system of drainage, and being concerned in the improvement of the outfall, as engineer to the General Commissioners, reccommended Mau⁓ ⌐oster as the outlet, but at the same time he distinctly stated ⋮   ⋮o efficient drainage for the lowlands could be obtained ther   ⋮ss the river was to be greatly improved by straightening   ⋮ening it, a measure which he urged very strongly on th   ⋮ion of Boston, and as this plan would effect a saving o.   ⋮28,000 as against that of making a new cut to Hobhole, he recommended that "the East Fen in consequence of this saving should contribute liberally to the improvement of Boston Haven; and also that as the waters of the West and Wildmore Fens would also obtain a better outfall, it should be a consideration whether they also should not contribute to the expense."

These reports being brought before the Corporation, they expressed their willingness to contribute one-half the expense of straightening the river from Maud Foster to Hobhole, as recommended by Mr. Rennie. This was not deemed sufficient by the Drainage Commissinners, and finally, after a great deal of consideration of the several schemes, they determined that the water from the uplands and the West and Wildmore Fens should be conducted to Maud Foster, but that the outfall of the drainage from the sock and downfall of the East fen should be near Fishtoft Gowt. This decision failed to give general satisfaction, and one pamphleteer, in a letter addressed to the Commissioners, asks how many *pails* of water they expect will pass down Maud Foster Drain, and observes, "If this drain is executed upon the proposed dimensions, from the sluice to Cowbridge, there will not be a supply of water to cover that drain above one inch deep."

The scheme being settled, an Act was obtained in 1801 " for the better and more effectually draining certain tracts of land, called Wildmore Fen and the West and East Fens, in the county of Lincoln, and also the low lands and grounds in the several parishes, townships, and places, having right of common in the said fens, and other lowlands and grounds lying contiguous or adjoining thereto." By this act the boundaries of the Fourth District of the Witham Commissioners were extended, and made to include the East Fen and the lowlands in Wrangle. This area was still further enlarged by a subsequent Act in 1818, 58 Geo. III., cap ix., and the lowlands in Great Steeping, Thorpe, Irby,

Firsby, Bratoft, Croft, and Wainfleet All Saints added. The Act obtained in 1801 was amended by another Act in 1803, and again in 1818.

Under the powers of these Acts the following works were executed for the drainage of the fens by Mr. Rennie.

The highland water was taken up by a catchwater drain skirting the boundary of the East Fen. This drain commenced near Little Steeping, and discharged its waters into the West Fen catchwater drain at Cherry Corner. Its length is about seven miles, and its bottom was made to an inclined plane of six inches fall per mile.

The lowland waters were provided for by a new cut, commencing near Toynton, passing through the centre of the East Fen, and discharging at Hobhole, where a sluice was built, the cill of which was laid five feet below that of the Grand Sluice, or two feet below the then average of low water spring tides in the river. It has three openings of fifteen feet each, and the drain, from its outfall to the junction at Freiston Common, was made with a bottom forty feet wide, diminishing gradually from that point to twelve feet at its termination, near Toynton St. Peter's. The length of the cut is fourteen miles, and it was laid out with a fall of five inches per mile.

The following new cuts were also made in connection with Hobhole Drain :—Barlode Drain was cleaned out, deepened, and extended, and made to communicate with Hobhole Drain at a point opposite White Cross Drain, and running thence in a westerly direction till it joined the catchwater drain : this was made sixteen feet wide. Lade Bank Drain was scoured and deepened and enlarged to a ten feet bottom, from North Dyke Bridge to the Main Drain, and thence continued in an easterly direction along the Fen Dyke bank to lands in the parish of Friskney. Steeping River was straightened, widened, deepened, and embanked, so as to prevent its flooding the low lands; as also the Great Steeping Beck, and the several sewers and drains in connection.

For the drainage of the West and Wildmore Fens a catchwater drain was made, skirting the adjacent high lands. It commences near the junction of the river Bane with the Witham, in the parish of Coningsby, and passing through Tumby, Mareham, and Revesby, to Hagnaby, thence turns south to Cowbridge, receiving the East Fen catchwater at Cherry Corner. From this point it was intended that it should continue, by a distinct cut, with thirty feet bottom, parallel with Maud Foster to the Haven, and discharge at a new sluice to be built at the side of Maud Foster, so that the high and low land waters should have separate outlets; but by the amended Act, obtained in 1803, the Commissioners were authorised to omit the making of the new cut from Cowbridge to the Haven and the erection of the additional sluice, and instead to make the existing arrangement by which the upland waters flow to sea by means of Maud Foster Drain, and provision made as hereafter described for the West Fen waters to flow into Hobhole, when over-ridden by them. This catchwater drain is about eighteen miles in length, and the bottom was made to an inclined plane rising six inches in the mile. The width of the bottom, at the lower end, is eighteen feet, diminishing gradually to eight feet at its commencement near Coningsby.

The old Maud Foster Gowt was pulled down, and a new sluice built, with three openings of thirteen feet four inches each; the cill being laid one foot nine inches below that of the Grand Sluice. The drain was deepened and widened to Cowbridge, the bottom being made thirty feet wide, and rising six inches per mile. Across this drain, at Cowbridge, a sluice is erected, with pointing doors to prevent the water from the high lands, which discharges below this point, from backing up into the fens. Above the doors a communication is made to admit the West and Wildmore Fen waters into Hobhole Drain when they are above the gauge weir, and in danger of flooding the low lands. This drain, called New Dyke, passes under the catchwater drain, the waters of which are conveyed over it by a stone aqueduct, having three arches or openings of twelve feet each, and joins Hobhole Drain at Freiston Common. There was a stop or weir above the aqueduct, made to a proper height for the purpose of sending all the water that was possible through Maud Foster Gowt at ordinary times; but as soon as the water rose within two feet of the surface of the lowlands it ran over the weir. In times of flood, when the water was within one foot of the medium surface of the lowest lands, the doors were opened and the water allowed to flow freely to Hobhole. There is also a side cut near this place, in which is a lock to allow of the passage of boats from the West Fen to Hobhole Drain.

This restriction as to the passage of the waters out of the West Fen through New Dyke into Hobhole Drain was withdrawn in the Act obtained in the session of 1867, and the Commissioners have power now to allow the stop doors to remain open for the six winter months, so that the West Fen waters will be discharged at Hobhole instead of at Maud Foster as formerly.

From Cowbridge the drainage is provided for by the West Fen drain, which is a straight cut, with a thirty-feet bottom, as far as the junction with Medlam drain, at Mount Pleasant, where it turns to the west and joins Newham drain; thence along Howbridge drain to the end thereof, at Little Wildmore, near Dogdyke, where the bottom was made only eight feet wide. It has an average inclination throughout its whole length of about nine and a half miles of five inches per mile. Medlam Drain is the principal outlet for the West Fen, commencing at the West Fen

Drain, at Mount Pleasant, and extending to Revesby. It was made eighteen feet in width at the bottom, diminishing gradually to twelve feet at its upper end. The length is upwards of six miles, and the bottom has a rise of five inches per mile. There is another cut for the purpose of draining the south part of Wildmore Fen, commencing at the West Fen Drain, at Cowbridge, and extending on the south side of Frith Bank enclosure to Anton Gowt into Newham Drain, and thence along Castle Dyke and Long Dyke Drains. This drain was made sixteen foot in width at the bottom, at its junction with the West Fen Drain, diminishing to eight feet at the upper end. The length is about eight miles, and the rate of inclination was laid out at four and a half inches per mile. There are several other small drains for the purpose of collecting the surface water and conveying it into the mains, which it is not necessary to describe.

The general surface of the lowlands in the West Fen was, at the time of the completion of the drainage, about eleven feet above the cill of Maud Foster Sluice, but a portion of the surface of Wildmore Fen was a foot lower than this. The surface of the highest part of the East Fen was about the same level, but a great deal of it was a foot lower, and the lowest parts, formerly the Deeps, were only nine feet above Hobhole cill.

To meet the expenses of carrying out and maintaining these works the General Commissioners were authorised to levy additional rates on Wildmore and the West Fens, to the extent of fourpence per acre, so long as they remained common lands; but on their enclosure, the rate might be raised to one shilling per acre. On the East Fen a tax of one shilling per acre was imposed on the lands held in severalty—eightpence per acre on half-year lands, and fourpence on common lands, to be raised to one shilling on their enclosure. They were also authorised to enclose and sell six hundred acres of the common land, the proceeds to be applied towards the cost of the drainage.

For carrying out the improvement of the Steeping river, the estimated expense of which, together with other works incidental thereto, amounted to £28,914 ; the proprietors of the land liable to be flooded were to contribute the sum of £18,627, to be assessed on their lands, and the General Commissioners, on receipt of this sum, were to execute the whole of the works.

The first stone of Hobhole sluice was laid March 7th, 1805, and it was opened September 3rd, 1806. The first stone of the new Maud Foster sluice was laid 21st of May, 1806, and the sluice was opened the following year.

Acts of Parliament were subsequently obtained for the enclosure of the common lands, (41 Geo. III., cs. 100, 141, 142, Acts for Enclosing the Wildmore and East and West Fens ; 42 Geo. III. c. 108 ; 50 Geo. III, c. 129.) A certain portion was decreed to the impropriators in lieu of tithes ; the Duchy of Lancaster took a twentieth part in lieu of manorial rights ; another portion was set apart for churches and roads ; and the remainder awarded to the proprietors of toftsteads and lands within the respective parishes.

Fourteen thousand acres of land sold by the Commissioners, acting under the powers of the Enclosure Acts, together with other extra parochial lands, were subsequently formed (52 Geo.III. c. 144) into seven separate townships called respectively East Ville, Midville, Frithville, Carrington, Westville, Thornton-le-Fen, and Langriville.

The allotted roads were at first maintained and repaired by the several townships through which they pased, certain land having been awarded by the Commissioners for supplying the materials ; but subsequently, disputes having arisen, some of the new parishes refused to maintain and repair them, and consequently the roads became utterly neglected and almost impassable. In winter time the ruts were so deep that no light conveyance could safely pass over the roads, and it was not an uncommon occurrence for vehicles to become so embedded in the mud that the driver had to seek the assistance of some neighbouring farmer to extricate his waggon with the aid of several horses. This state of things remained in this condition till within the last thirteen years, when on its being decided that the award of the Commissioners who had allotted the land for the roads and for their repairs was inoperative, as they had exceeded their powers, an Act of Parliament was obtained for the better regulation and maintenance of the highways. Previous to this being done, it had been attempted by an indictment against one of the parishes, through which the roads passed, to compel the parishes to repair them; but the case being carried to the Court of Queen's Bench, the decision was given in favour of the Parish. Several influential owners and occupiers of land in the neighbourhood then met together and determined to put an end to this disgraceful state of affairs, and in 1853 an Act, 16 and 17 Vic., cap. 115, was obtained " for the better maintenance and repair of the highways in Wildmore and the East and West Fens," by which it was enacted that the whole of the roads set out under the enclosure awards as public ways should be deemed highways, and be made subject to the same laws and regulations as governed the highways throughout the country.

The drainage of the fens, as already narrated, was completely effective. Mr. Bower, reporting to the Bedford Level Corporation, in 1814, says : " It is satisfactory to state that every wished-for object in the drainage of the whole of the fens and of the low lands adjoining is effectually obtained, and the lowest land brought into a state of cultivation. The East Fen deeps are so perfectly drained, and so confident are the proprietors of this, that part of them now forms a considerable farm-yard; but stronger proofs of this than mere assertion have now been had. There have been within the last five years several extraordinary floods and high tides, which have not in the smallest degree affected the works or low lands; and at this moment of time, when the low lands in every part of the kingdom are overflowed by an ice flood, the East, West, and Wildmore Fens and low lands adjoining are perfectly free, and as ready for all agricultural purposes as the high country lands." However true this statement may have been at the time it was written it is scarcely correct now. Two causes have conduced to the alteration. By the complete drainage of the spongy soil of the East Fen, and its consolidation by working, the surface has subsided from one to two feet. On the other hand, the channel of the outfall from Hobhole to the deeps has been raised from its former level by the deposit of silt, arising from the general encroachment of the sands on the sea on this coast, and the neglect of proper training works. To such an extent has this occurred that low water level of spring tides which, at the time of the erection of Hobhole sluice, stood only two feet on the cill, now is constantly from six to seven feet, and in times of flood as much as eight and even ten feet; so that, owing to the subsidence of the land on the one hand and the deterioration of the outfall on the other, the good effects originally felt by this drainage are in a great measure neutralised, and in wet seasons the low lands are liable to be flooded and the crops destroyed.

In the winter of 1866 a long continued and heavy downfall of rain clearly demonstrated the system of drainage in its present condition to be quite inadequate to the discharge of the water. A very large area of land in the East Fen was for many weeks completely under water. Viewed from Keal-hill the level was described as having the appearance of one extensive lake, the course of the drains being undistinguishable from the submerged lands. Occupiers, in some cases, had even to use boats to pass from one part of the farm to the other, and the roots stored in the fields were rendered quite inaccessible.

So far back as 1861 Mr. Hawkshaw was applied to by the General Commissioners to advise them on the drainage of this district, and requested to devise a plan for draining the Fourth District, and also an alternative scheme, which, while improving this particular tract of land, would also be more general in its application. In 1865 Mr. Welsh, the surveyor to the Commissioners, was also directed to report to them on the drainage of the Fourth District. From these reports it appears that the Fourth District, including the East, West, and Wildmore Fens, and Five Thousand Acres, has a taxable area of 57,200 acres.

About 25,000 acres of land in the East Fen, and 15,000 in the West and Wildmore Fens, are below ordinary flood level; and while the larger portion of the West and Wildmore Fens, and the land draining into Hobhole Drain below Lade Bank, are comparatively uninjured by the water in the drains, rising to eleven feet above the cill of Hobhole Sluice, a considerable portion of the East Fen lying to the north of Lade Bank is, when the water rises to that height, incapable of being drained by gravitation to Hobhole. The portion of the East Fen, including lands draining into it, which extend north of Lade Bank, amounts to about 30,000 acres. About one-half of this quantity lies at so low a level as to require for its effectual drainage that the water at Hobhole should not rise higher than about seven feet above the cill; but that level is one foot below low water of the Witham outside of Hobhole Sluice in times of flood, which then rises to eight feet above the cill, and it is for this reason that these low lands cannot on those occasions drain naturally by Hobhole.

The general scheme recommended by Mr. Hawkshaw will be referred to fully in another chapter; it is not necessary, therefore, to make further allusion to it here. The local plan he advised was placing draw doors across Hobhole Drain, near Lade

Bank bridge, and the erection of a pumping engine of 180 horsepower at that spot to lift the flood waters from the northern to the southern side of the doors; the maximum of the lift being assumed at five feet, and the extreme effect on the drain below the doors—the raising of the water during the time the sea doors were shut by the tides eighteen inches; the estimated cost being £15,000 for engines, pumps, draw-doors, land, and works, and £3000 parliamentary expenses, &c.; the annual outlay for interest and repayment of principal money borrowed, spread over 35 years, being taken at £1350, and for working expenses and maintenance £1250, together £2600, equal to a tax of about eleven pence over the whole district for the first 35 years, and of twopence per acre afterwards. This scheme having been fully considered at a meeting of the Commissioners held in July, 1861, it was then resolved:—1. That a *general* plan improving all drainage is preferable to a local one; and also that a natural drainage is preferable to an artificial one. 2. That the Fourth District ought not to pay towards the general plan a sum larger than it would have to expend for its own local drainage. 3. That if the benefit is, as Mr. Hawkshaw anticipates, distributed to all the lands in the Fourth District, all the lands should pay according to the actual benefit received (the rate to be left to arbitration, the maximum being fixed at three shillings and the minimum at fourpence per acre). . . . . 10. That it would be desirable first to attempt to carry out the general plan. 11. That in the event of the other parties interested not being able or willing to carry out their share of the expenses of the general plan, then it would be expedient to have recourse to Mr. Hawkshaw's proposed local plan of draining the district by steam power.

Notwithstanding these resolutions the matter remained in abeyance until the year 1866, when the Fourth District Commissioners, despairing of any general scheme being carried out, decided on applying to Parliament for the necessary powers to enable them to erect a pumping engine at Lade Bank for the relief of the East Fen north of that point; and for the better drainage of the West and Wildmore Fens by the removal of the restriction placed on the stop-doors at Cowbridge, so that the water should be allowed to run freely out of the West Fen drain by Newdyke or Junction drain to Hobhole. And also for power to raise the sum of £20,000 on mortgage to pay for the works, and to levy a tax, not exceeding sixpence per acre, on the land, in addition to the two shillings on the West and Wildmore Fens, and one shilling on the East Fen, already sanctioned by former Acts. The Witham Drainage Act, 1867, received the royal assent on the 15th July, 1867.

Some objection was raised to this scheme at the time, on the ground that the greater portion of the land, the waters from which would have to be raised by steam power, was at so high a level as to render such a process perfectly unnecessary, and it was contended that means should be devised for separating the water of the East Fen proper from that of the Five Thousand Acres and the Steeping District, which lies considerably above it. Mr. Welsh, in his report, had advised that these waters should be cut off from the pumps by stopping the Bell Water Drain where the railway crosses it, and that they should be conveyed thence to Fountain's Sewer by a new cut along the side of the railway, and thence to Hobhole Drain by Fountain's Sewer, enlarged. Mr. David Martin, also, in a pamphlet addressed to the Commissioners, recommended that Bell-water Drain should be made a catch-water for conveying these high-land waters to the sea, and that a new drain should be cut on the west side of Hobhole Drain, from Fodder Dyke Drain to Bardolph Drain, with other alterations in the arrangements of the several sewers, so that the waters from the lower part of the East Fen might be conveyed to an engine to be erected on the west bank of Hobhole, about half way between Fodder Dyke and Bardolph. By carrying out this scheme the engines might have been of much less power, and having less work to do, an annual saving in working expenses would be effected; but then on the other hand it was deemed that the increased outlay in purchase of land, and the annual interest, would make the result in the end nearly the same. Mr. Hawkshaw's plan was therefore carried out as originally devised.

The new Pumping works are situated at Lade Bank, on the west side of Hobhole Drain, on lands formerly belonging to Hunston's Charity. They consist of two pairs of high pressure condensing steam engines, working two of Appold's centrifugal pumps. The fan of each pump is of brass, seven feet in diameter, driven by a wrought-iron, vertical shaft and bevil pinion wheel, and is connected to one pair of engines. The diameter of the cylinders of the engines is thirty inches, and the stroke thirty inches. The steam is supplied by six Cornish boilers, each twenty-three feet long and six feet five inches in diameter, the safe pressure being sixty pounds on the inch. One pump and its pair of engines forms a complete and independent machine, calculated to lift the water six feet above the drainage level. The pumps, engines, and boilers are contained in two large brick buildings, with iron roofs covered with slates, the pump races being directly under the engines. The chimney shaft is twelve feet square at the base and ninety feet in height, finished at the top with stone corbels, and a cast iron ornamental cap weighing three tons.

The dam across the drain consists of two sluices, with self-acting doors pointing down the drain, with a lock in the centre. The lock is seventy feet long and twelve feet wide; the total water way, being thirty-six feet. These works, as well as the foundations for the engines, are constructed of bricks laid in hydraulic lime,

FEN SLODGERS.

and coped with Bramley Fall stone. The contract for the works was taken by Messrs. Easton and Amos, of London, and they have been carried out under the superintendence of Mr. H. C. Anderson, the cost being £17,000.

There is no doubt that the benefit to the occupiers of land in the East Fen from these works will be very considerable;— the payment of the small additional tax of sixpence per acre required towards the expenses of working the engines, and the repayment of the money borrowed, will bear no comparison to the annual loss sustained by the destruction of crops from the constant flooding to which this fen has been subject. The passing of the West Fen waters, also, by the way of Hobhole drain will greatly facilitate the discharge of the drainage from the West Fen, yet it can only be regarded as a matter of expediency. The diversion of waters from their ancient outfall at Maud Foster sluice, to a point much lower down the river, militates against a general principle, which teaches that for the preservation or improvement of a tidal river, the tributary streams should be conducted to its channel at the highest possible point. The introduction of steam power also for the main drainage of the East Fen must be regarded as an unfortunate precedent. The principle by which the engineers were guided in laying out the drainage of the fens of this district was that of gravitation, and there is no doubt that this system would be fully effective if only a good outfall were secured. The diversion of funds to the erection of these engines adds to the already numerous difficulties in bringing about a joint scheme affecting the whole drainage of the district by an improvement of the outfall, and seems to place the accomplishment of that object at a greater distance than ever.

CHAPTER IV.

THE BLACK SLUICE DISTRICT.

The district included in the above heading is all that area of land which pays taxes to the Black Sluice Commissioners; consisting of the 2nd and 5th Witham districts, Holland Fen, and what Dugdale calls the Lyndsey Level. It is bounded on the north by Kyme Eau, the river Witham, and the town of Boston; on the east by the high lands in the parishes of Skirbeck Quarter, Wyberton, Kirton, Swineshead, Donington, Gosberton, and Pinchbeck; on the south by the Glen and Bourn Eau; and on the west by the Car Dyke, which passes near to Bourn, Rippingale, Billingborough, Horbling, Helpringham, and Heckington. The taxable area is 64,395 acres, but the total quantity of land which discharges its water into the Witham, through the Black Sluice, is about 134,351.

The outlet for the drainage of this district is at the Black Sluice, in Skirbeck Quarter. The main drain is the South Forty Foot river; which runs through the centre of the fen, and is 21 miles in length; receiving throughout its course the contents of about 30 other drains, the principal of which are the North Forty Foot, the Clay dyke and the Old Hammond beck.

According to Dugdale, the first mention made of this portion of the fens occurs in the reign of Henry I., who made it a royal forest, in which condition it remained until Richard I., by his charter to the monastery of Spalding of the towns of Spalding and Pinchbeck, with the lands, waters, and marshes to them belonging, did acquit the inhabitants of those places from all duties belonging to the forests; as also of harts and hinds with all other wild beasts; and of all forest customs and exactions which used to be there done or required ; so that no forester or any other might thereupon vex or disquiet them ; and moreover, gave them licence to make banks and ditches to inclose their lands and marshes; and also to build houses, and exercise tillage as they themselves should think fit.

In Henry the Third's reign, an order was made by the King that, after the boundaries were properly fixed, the Hauthunter (Holland) Fen, extending from Swineshead to Dogdyke, should be divided, with the consent of those who had right therein ; and subsequently, in the 44th year of his reign, the King, "directing his precept to the Shirereeve of the county, whereby taking notice that not only the landowners in those parts, but himself, had suffered inestimable damage by the overflowing of the sea, and likewise of the fresh waters, through the default in the repairs of the banks, ditches, gutters, bridges, and sewers in the lands which lately belonged to William Longespe, in the Parts of Kesteven and Holland, he commanded the said Shire-reeve forthwith to distrain all such landholders who had safeguard by those banks and ditches, and ought to repair them according to the proportion of their lands, to the end that they might be speedily repaired in such sort as they ought and had used."

In Edward the Second's reign a commission was appointed to view the fens. They made a survey and presentment as to the whole of the banks and drains, minutely setting out their condition, and whose duty it was to repair and maintain them ; from which it appears that the northern part of the level drained into Kyme Eau by means of a river called Bridgefleet, the cleaning and repairing of which belonged to the town of Heckington as far as the river at Swineshead, the channel being sufficient to carry the water down to Kyme Mouth. The rest of Holland Fen drained by a sewer, called the Encluse, near Boston, three feet in width, which discharged near the west end of the bridge, and also by the Hammond beck, which was kept in repair by Boston and Skirbeck Quarter; in consideration whereof the men of Boston, living at the west end of the said bridge, had common rights in the marsh of the Eight-hundreds. The rest of the sewer, extending to Blalberdeboche, Swinesheved, and Byker, was to be repaired by the town of Swineshead. The other sewers then in existence, and the places liable to their repair, were as follows:—The Swyneman dam and Swane-lade, 16 to 20 feet wide passing near Donington, Quadring, and Gosberton, to Bicker Haven, and repaired by those parishes; Risegate Ees (Rysegate Eau), extending from Gosberton to the sea, belonging to the parish of Gosberton; the sewer of the Beche, running from Pinchbeck north fen to the sea, belonging to the parishes of Pinchbeck and Surfleet; Burne Aldo Ee (Bourn Old Eau), running from Bourn through Surfleet to the sea; the first portion from Bourn to Gutheram cote, belonging to the town and the Abbot of Bourn jointly; and thence the Surfleet, belonging to the town of Pinchbeck, and after that to Surfleet. Dunsby was drained by a sewer called the Soud; Hacconby, by one called Fenbrigg.

After this several commissions were issued to view the state of the fens and fix the boundaries, the particulars of which are only a recapitulation of the above.

In 25 Edward III. a petition was presented to the King and his council in Parliament, by the inhabitants of the fens in Kesteven and Holland, showing that the ancient boundary between the two divisions of the county, the Mid-fen dyke, and the other metes which went through the said fens from the Welland to the Witham, were at that time, by reason of floods and other impediments, so obscured as to be no longer visible, and hence frequent quarrels occurred between the inhabitants: in consequence a commission was appointed, the boundaries properly set out, and defined by stone crosses.

About this time also a presentment was exhibited against the town of Bourn, with the hamlet of Dyke and Calthorp, and the town of Morton and Hermethorpe, for turning the fresh water towards the north, through the fens to Boston, instead of allowing it to run eastwards towards the sea.

In the 41st year of Edward the Third's reign, a dispute occurred between the Abbots of Peterborough and Swineshead as to the ownership of some marsh land in Gosberton, supposed to be part of Bicker Haven, a full account of which will be found in the chapter on the history of the Court of Sewers.

In Henry the Eighth's time the first systematic attempt at drainage was made, a Commission of Sewers was appointed and sat at Donington, and having made survey of the fen, decreed that two great sewers, 20 feet wide and 5 feet deep, running parallel at a distance of 36 feet from each other, should be cut from Gutheram's Cote to a point called Wragmere Stake, where they were to unite and continue in one channel 30 feet wide to Gill syke, and then to the river Witham at Langrick, where was a sluice. "And the said waters from the rivers of Glen to Witham, so intended from the south to the north, should fall into, enter, and go through all the lodes and drains in the fens aforesaid which came out of the parts of Kesteven to Hammond Beck, to the end that all the waters going together might the better run within its own brinks and channels, and the sooner come to the sluice at Skirbeck Gote, and the new gotes at Langrick." At Langrick a new sluice was to be built of freestone, with four doors, each eight feet wide. The sewers were to be paid for by the several parishes through which the drains passed, and the sluice by the fen towns in Kesteven, Heckington, Kyme, and Ewerby.

This order of the Court of Sewers was disobeyed by the parishes, who, instead of performing the works severally required of them, disputed the power of the Commission to make order for the execution of new works of drainage, contending that their functions only extended to the maintenance of the old and existing works. And so matters remained in abeyance till Queen Elizabeth's time, in the 8th year of whose reign a Court of Sewers was held at Sempringham, and a general tax was again laid for carrying out the works ordered by the former court; but nothing was done until nine years afterwards. At another court held at Swineshead, the country complained that they were drowned more than formerly; and upon this an order was again made that those drains which the Duke of Suffolk and others had ordained to be begun about the latter end of King Henry the Eighth's time, as also some others, should forthwith be set upon, and a tax was laid to pay for the same. The towns again refused to pay, and nothing was done for twenty-seven years, when the case was brought before the Court of Queen's Bench. Dugdale gives the following account of the trial:—

"In 43 and 44 Elizabeth a great controversy did arise in the county of Lincoln about the erecting of two new gotes at Skirbeck and Langare, for draining the waters of South Holland and the fens into Boston Haven, which work Sir Edward Dimock, Knight, did by himself and his friends further what he could, but it was opposed by the county of Kesteven; and the exception taken thereto was that the Commissioners of Sewers could not, by the power of their commission, make a law for the erecting of these new gotes where never any stood before; whereupon the decision of this point coming at length before the then two Justices, viz., Popham and Anderson, they delivered their opinions that the said new gotes, if they were found to be good and profitable for the safety and advantage of the country, they might be erected by the power of this statute."

Notwithstanding this judgment the inhabitants could not be made to pay, and the works were never carried out. In Charles the First's reign three of the Commissioners of Sewers, one of whom was Sergeant Callis, the author of the standard work on the Law of Sewers, made a representation to the King that all this fen was surrounded with water, and had no cattle on it, and praying him to take some steps for its reclamation; whereupon special courts were held at Sleaford and Boston in the year 1638, and an order was made for the draining of the fens, a tax of 13s. 4d. per acre being laid upon the land to pay for the same. The landowners still refusing to pay, three years afterwards, upon the direction of the King, the Commissioners, at courts held at Sleaford, Swineshead, Boston, and Bourn, made a contract with the Earl of Lindsey, Lord High Chamberlain of England, to drain the fens lying between Kyme Eau and the Glen, computed to contain 36,000 acres; for doing which he was to receive 24,000 acres of the reclaimed land, taken proportionately out of the several fens. Whereupon the Earl of Lindsey set vigorously to work, and completed the drainage so effectually that three years afterwards, at a Court of Sewers held at Sleaford, after survey made of the sluices, banks, and sewers, decree was made that the Earl had made full performance of his contract, and the grant of land he was to receive as payment was ratified to him. The cost of this work was £45,000. On its completion the Earl and his fellow adventurers inclosed the fens, built houses and farmsteads, and brought the land into cultivation, and continued in peaceable possession for about three years.

About the same time (1638) King Charles himself undertook the drainage of the Eight Hundred, or Haut Huntre Fen, being that portion of the level lying east of Earl Lindsey's Fen, or between Langrick and Boston, computed to contain twenty-two thousand acres; and a tax of twenty shillings the acre was levied upon the inhabitants of Brothertoft, Swineshead, Wigtoft, Sutterton, Algarkirk, Fosdyke, Kirton, Frampton, Wyberton, Hale, Dogdyke, and Boston claiming common therein. On this tax not being paid, the Commissioners of Sewers, at a court held at Boston, declared the King to be the sole undertaker for the draining thereof, and as recompense of the cost of the same, granted to him eight thousand acres of the reclaimed land. The King parted with his interest to Sir William Killigrew, who was also a fellow adventurer with the Earl of Lindsey in his drainage of the rest of the level; and under his direction this fen was drained and reclaimed. A gote was built in Skirbeck Quarter on the site of the old Black Sluice, and a new cut made as far as Swineshead. The Lindsey level was drained by a cut made from Gutheram's Cote to Swineshead, pursuing the course of the present South Forty Foot; by straightening and scouring out the old Hammond Beck; and by cutting lateral drains through the adjacent fens to the high land.

The Earl and his partner, Sir W. Killigrew, were successful with the drainage, and the country began to assume a habitable appearance, but several disputes as to the rights of the adventurers to their share of the reclaimed land having arisen, petitions were presented to Parliament by the fen men. After an enquiry, orders were granted by both Houses confirming the Earl in the possession of his property. The malcontents, thus failing to obtain their way, in contempt of all law and order, destroyed the drains and buildings, and also the crops—then ready to be reaped—to a very great value; and up to Dugdale's time (1662) had "held possession, to the great decay and ruin of those costly works and exceeding discommodity to all that part of the country." They also attempted to pull down the new sluice at Boston, which had cost £6000. Sir Wm. Killigrew appealed to the Mayor of Boston, and prayed that an order might be given " to enquire out those that are now pulling that great sluice to pieces, which if it should, by this breaking up, be suncke by the water getting under it, the sea will break in all that side of the country, where no sea ever came. By the ruin of this our main sluice I conseave a hundred thousand pound damage may be done to the country, which those rogues doe not consider that doe steale and breake up the iron and the plankes of that great Sluse."

It does not appear that the adventurers could procure any relief: the unsettled state of public affairs, party spirit, and other causes growing out of the circumstances of the period, seem to have impeded the course of justice, and Sir William died forty years after his petition to Parliament a poor man, ruined by his adventure. For nearly a hundred years the fen remained unreclaimed. Some idea may be gained of its condition from the following description given by Mr. Thompson :—" The whole of the land between Brothertoft and Boston was frequently overflowed during the winter season. The turnpike road from Boston to Swineshead, and the intersecting roads leading to the adjacent villages were covered with a considerable depth of water ; of course they were dangerous to travel upon, and the country people brought their produce to Boston market in boats, being enabled very frequently to come in them as far as Rosegarth corner in West-street, the water often reaching to the White Horse inn in that street."

In the year 1765, being the fifth year of the reign of George III., the owners of the lands in the Holland Fen and the Lyndsey level bestirred themselves, and determined to make another attempt to reclaim these fens. They accordingly applied to Parliament and obtained an Act under the title of " an Act (v. Geo. III., cap. 85) for draining and improving certain low marsh and fen lands lying between Boston Haven and Bourn, in the parts of Kesteven and Holland, in the county of Lincoln." By this Act the management of the district was taken out of the jurisdiction of the Court of Sewers, and was given to a commission consisting of all persons who possessed property in the fen to the value of £100 per annum, or were heirs apparent to property of the value of £100 per annum, and who should qualify themselves by taking the oath prescribed by the Act. Power was granted to do works, and levy taxes not exceeding 9d. per acre on the lowest lands, 4½d. on the higher level, and 3d. on Holland Fen. In order to prevent the work being rendered abortive, as all previous attempts had been, by the lawlessness of the fen men, it was made a *felony* to injure or destroy any of the banks, sluices, or drains, and persons found guilty of such acts were liable to seven years' transportation. This clause was repealed in the 12th year of the present reign, when the good effects of the drainage being felt by all, the common sense of the inhabitants became sufficient protection to the works without the infliction of so heavy a penalty, and in lieu thereof persons injuring any of the works became liable to a penalty of £5.

The following were the works authorised and carried out under the powers of this and subsequent Acts, and the regulations imposed on the Commissioners as to the neighbouring banks and water courses :—The heightening and strengthening the north bank of the river Glen and Bourn Eau from Dove Hurn or Pinchbeck Bars to Bourn ; erecting a new sluice at the lower end of the South Forty Foot Drain, on the spot where the old Black Sluice formerly stood, the water way to be fifty-six feet, or as nearly the dimensions of the old sluice as possible, the sluice to have four pairs of doors; the South Forty Foot Drain to be lowered from the sluice to Clay Dyke, and to have sixty feet top and forty-six feet bottom as far as Hale Fen, then thirty feet bottom ; a new main drain to be made from the South Forty Foot to Gutheram's Cote, with thirty feet bottom, decreasing to ten feet at the upper end ; to scour out and widen New Hammond Beck from Redstone Gowt to its junction with the Forty Foot, the Old Hammond Beck throughout its length, and other minor drains.

The Deeping Fen proprietors were to be exonerated from keeping in repair the North Bank of the Glen, from Dove Hurn to Gutheram's Cote, and the Black Sluice Commissioners to maintain the same; the Deeping Fen proprietors paying £18 per annum. They were also to keep in repair the bank from this point to the high lands in Bourn, this parish and Cawthorpe and the other proprietors of the bank paying at the rate of twenty shillings a furlong for the maintenance of the same.

The state of Bourn Eau and the river Glen have been a constant cause of anxiety to the managers of the Black Sluice district. The bed of the latter river gradually rose so high, by accumulated deposits, as to make the drainage by it very imperfect and render the banks liable to breaches from heavy floods. These banks have given way no less than seven times since the beginning of the present century, five of the breaches being on the south, and two on the north side; and in consequence several thousand acres of land were inundated, to the very serious loss of the occupiers. It has been stated that the cost, during this period, of maintaining the banks and repairing the breaches amounted to ten thousand pounds.

The banks of Bourn Eau were even in a worse condition than those of the Glen, being low and made of light and porous earth. For their preservation doors were placed at Tongue-end, pointing to the Glen, to prevent the water in floods reverting up the Bourn Eau; and an overfall, of about twenty feet in length, was fixed in the north bank to let part of the water into the fen when it should rise so high as to threaten a breach of the banks. This arrangement still continues, and the overflow is connected with the South Forty-foot river near Gutheram's Cote.

The amount authorised to be raised not proving sufficient, an amended Act (10 Geo. III., cap. 41) was obtained authorising the Commissioners to double the former taxes, which consequently became on the respective districts eighteen-pence, nine-pence, and sixpence per acre. They also obtained powers to carry out additional works, and to contribute three thousand pounds towards cleansing, deepening, and widening the Glen from the Sluice at the Reservoir to Tongue-end, on the Commissioners of Deeping Fen spending a similar amount.

The last attempt to drain the level was thoroughly successful. The works were efficiently carried out, and being well-designed entirely answered the expectation of the promoters; the Fen, which, before the drainage, was little better than a morass, growing a coarse herbage and affording a scanty pasturage during the summer months, became rich arable and grass lands, and the annual value increased tenfold. This result was not obtained without several serious riots caused by the Fen men, the successors of those who had so effectually destroyed the works carried out by Earl Lindsey and all former adventurers. The inclosure was regarded by these men as an infringement of rights and privileges which they had long enjoyed. Very lawless excesses were committed in opposition to and destructive of the public works, and fences which were erected in the day-time, were frequently pulled down during the night. Several rather serious riots took place, and some lives were lost; and it was long before there was anything like a general acquiescence in the proceedings, and an admission that the enclosure promoted the general good, without any possible infringement of individual rights.

The common effect on all fen lands by improved drainage is a general subsidence of the soil. The rapid abstraction of the water from the land into the drains causes the spongy soil gradually to consolidate, and this process is still further assisted by the ploughing and working of the land. The organic matter also which has accumulated on the surface, during many centuries, by being exposed to the atmosphere, decomposes, and the general result is a lowering of the level of the surface of the ground, in some places to an extent of two or even three feet. The great attention which has been paid of late years to the science of drainage, rendered necessary an improvement in the works which had formerly been deemed sufficient for the protection of the fen, and the general subsidence of the land, owing to the causes above referred to, made it necessary that the main drains should be dug to a lower level. The Commissioners, therefore, consulted Mr. Rennie, who being thoroughly convinced of the imperfection of any system of interior drainage without a proper outfall, never lost any opportunity of urging this self-evident fact on the various bodies of Commissioners with which he had to deal; and who in this instance acting on his advice, applied to the Corporation of Boston and the Witham Commissioners to join with them in a general scheme for the improvement of the Haven, but these Trusts having declined to do so, Mr. Rennie was directed to confine his attention to the internal drainage of the Black Sluice Level.

Mr. Rennie's report, dated September 19th, 1815, after referring to the inadequacy of the then means of drainage, by which cause a great deal of the land was frequently flooded and seriously injured, traced the cause to the great quantity of water which came into the fen from the high lands; and he considered that no effectual drainage could be obtained unless the waters which came from a higher level could be prevented from mixing with the fen waters and overriding them. For this purpose he recommended that the old Car dyke should be scoured out and converted into a catch-water drain, so as to intercept all the flood water which comes down from the high lands lying between Bourn and Ewerby, and that this water should be carried by Heckington Cut and Gill Syke into the North Forty-foot, and so by this drain to a new sluice above Boston Bridge, where it would be discharged into the Witham. He also recommended the deepening and cleansing of several other drains, and the strengthening of the north bank of Bourn Eau, the total cost of the works being estimated at £66,160, viz. :—

	£	s.	d.
The catchwater drain from Bourn to the Witham, near to the Grand Sluice	35,832	0	0
A new Sluice for the same, of 30 feet water way, and a tunnel under the North Forty-foot	12,220	0	0
Scouring out the South Forty-foot, Hammond Beck, and Sundries	12,406	0	0
Barrier Bank at Bourn Eau	5,702	0	0
	£66,160	0	0

These recommendations of Mr. Rennie were not carried into effect, and the condition of the drainage became so bad, that the lower lands were continually flooded and the crops destroyed or greatly injured. The loss throughout the level was stated, in some seasons, to be £40,000, and the annual loss £20,000.

The proprietors of Bourn Fen, failing to obtain drainage by natural means, after considerable litigation with the Black Sluice Commissioners, obtained an Act enabling them to employ steam power, and an engine was erected near Gutheram Cote. Other parishes followed this example, and thus obtained an individual benefit at a very much greater aggregate cost than the expense of one general measure.

The work of improvement was hindered for some time by a division of opinion which existed as to the best method of effecting a natural drainage of the level, one party (headed by Mr. Kingsman Foster, a Commissioner,) contended that the proper outlet of the waters of the south part of the Fen was the river Welland. His plan was to deepen and widen the river Glen, and to divert the waters of the level into these two streams. This gentleman further complained of what he considered a great injustice which was inflicted on the taxpayers of the Black Sluice Level, owing to the fact of 30,000 acres of land lying on the east of the Hammond Beck, and under the jurisdiction of the Court of Sewers, discharging their waters into the drains of the Black Sluice level without being taxed towards the expenses of that Trust. He attributed the cause of this to the silting up of the outlets belonging to the Court of Sewers, which ought to have conveyed these waters to the Welland. The plan of drainage proposed by Mr. Foster and his remarks respecting the "Surreptitious Drainage" do not appear to have held weight with his brother Commissioners, and are only mentioned here as an incident in the History of the Drainage of the Level.

At last, in the year 1844, the Commissioners directed their engineer, Mr. Lewin, to make a report as to the best means of improving the drainage. In the following year they called in Sir John Rennie, and having adopted his report, determined to go to Parliament for fresh powers to raise money and carry out works. Both Sir John Rennie and Mr. Lewin strongly advocated the plan proposed to the Commissioners by Mr. Rennie in 1815, for the conversion of the Car-dyke into a catchwater or receiving drain for the water flowing on the level from the high lands between Bourn and Ewerby; but against this there appears to have been so strong a prejudice that Sir John was obliged to abandon it, and he therefore prepared an amended scheme, with which the Commissioners went to Parliament, but considerable opposition being raised by the upper districts, and owing to other causes, the bill was not carried. In the following Session the Commissioners again put in an appearance with Sir William Cubitt, as their engineer, and succeeded in obtaining an Act, entitled: (9th Vict., cap. 297) "An Act for better draining and improving certain low marsh and fen lands lying between Boston and Bourn, in the county of Lincoln, and for further improving the navigation through such lands." This Act recites that the general means of draining the lands had become very defective, in consequence whereof considerable losses in agricultural produce were frequently sustained, the recurrence of which might be prevented by improvements made in the drainage, and also that no provision having been made in the former Acts for the discharge of the debt incurred in carrying them into execution, this debt had for many years operated as an obstacle to the application of sufficient means for maintaining the existing works of drainage in an efficient state, and that it was therefore desirable to make arrangements for the gradual extinction of the existing and any future debts.

The works sanctioned by the Act were as follows :—

1. The lowering of the South Forty-foot river from end to end to a depth of from four to five feet on an average, so as to bring the bottom of the river at Gutheram Cote on a level with the existing cill of the Black Sluice, and to give a gradual inclination, or fall, at the rate of three inches per mile throughout its length.

2. The erection of a new sluice at a point a little south of the old Black Sluice, with three openings of the width of 20 feet clear (one being constructed for use as a navigation lock). The cills to be six feet below the cill of the existing sluice.

3. The scouring out and enlarging and deepening the Twenty-foot drain, and also the old skirth.

4. The Hammond beck from its junction with the Forty-foot to Dove Hurn to be deepened three feet on an average, so that its bottom at the junction should be six inches below the cill of the Black sluice; and to have an inclination at the rate of three inches per mile as far as the Twenty-foot drain in Gosberton Fen, and above that point at the rate of fourteen inches per mile.

5. Clay-dike, New-cut, Heckington Head-drain, Mid-fodder-drain, Hodge-dyke, and the several other drains, which belonged to the Commissioners, were to be scoured out and deepened, so as to correspond with the improved condition of the Forty-foot river.

In consideration that the maintenance of the north bank of the river Glen is essential for securing the level from partial inundation from the waters of that river, and that it would tend to the safety of this bank if the waters had a freer passage to the sea by means of its channel being scoured out and deepened and the cill of the Outlet Sluice lowered, the Commissioners were authorised to subscribe a sum, not exceeding two thousand pounds, towards the carrying out of such work; but if the persons having the management of the Glen did not undertake the improvement of the river, the Commissioners were at once to strengthen the North Bank of the river Glen and Bourn Eau.

Power was also given to the Trust to subscribe towards any works that might be carried out by the Boston Harbour Trustees, or others, for the improvement of the Haven; and also towards any works for scouring out or deepening Risegate Eau, or any other rivers or drains, provided such works would tend to accelerate the passage of the waters from the Black Sluice Level. New regulations were laid down for the management of the navigation and collection of toll, and several other matters relating to the internal administration of the Trust were provided for. Additional taxing powers were granted to meet the expenses of carrying the Act into execution. The extra rate for building the sluice was 2s. 6d. per acre on all lands in the level for a period not exceeding four years, and not raising a greater sum than £30,000. Bourn and Dike were liable to pay only 1s. 3d. per acre, in addition to the 1s. 6d. to which they were already liable. In addition to the 2s. 6d., extra taxes for five years, for paying for the improvement of the Forty-foot and other drains, were imposed on the level, in the following proportions: The several rates of 1s. 6d., 9d., and 6d. respectively, were doubled for a period of five years; at the expiration of this period the first-named district was to pay 2s., the second 1s., and the third 8d. per acre extra. Power was granted to raise money on mortgage not exceeding, in the whole, a sum of £80,000; but after the expiration of five years, arrangement was made for the extinction of the whole of the debt due by the Trust by the annual repayment of a sum of £1,200.

The time granted by this Act for the execution of the works and the funds provided not being sufficient, an amended Act (12 and 13 Vict., cap 59) was obtained in 1849, by which the district liable to the rate of eighteen-pence was charged with a capital tax of 2s. 3d.; the nine-penny district with 1s. 1½d., and the sixpenny with 9d. extra, until October, 1850; after that the extra tax on the first was to be reduced to 4½d., the second to 2¼d., and the third 1½d. Power was also taken to borrow an additional sum of £10,000. Under the power of these two Acts the works enumerated have been carried out, and the arterial drainage of the level rendered as perfect as engineering science can make it.

The numerous steam engines constantly at work pumping the water from the adjacent fens into the main drains, and the great height of water constantly standing on the cill of the Black Sluice, scarcely ever less than ten feet, shows there is yet room for considerable improvement; and as the Commissioners have done all that lies in their power to make their own arrangements perfect, and their drains and sluices are maintained in excellent order and repair, it is obvious than any remedy which is to be obtained must be sought for below the point of discharge of their waters. As they have powers to subscribe towards works for the improvement of Boston Haven, it is greatly to be hoped that some general arrangement may be come to, by all the interested trusts, by which a scheme for improving the outfall may be effectually carried out.

Complaints are occasionally made with respect to the working and condition of the interior drains. This no doubt arises from the representative system of management which has been adopted, and the consequent loss of advantage to be derived from having the whole system of outlet and interior drainage placed under one management. Each parish yearly nominates its own officer who receives his appointment from the Commissioners. The duty of this officer is to attend to the internal drains, or sewers, belonging to his Parish, and to collect the taxes. It has been found by constant experience, and is a principle which is rapidly gaining ground—as for instance in the Highway districts formed throughout the country—that all work requiring technical knowledge is better performed by a permanent officer, who is properly qualified by practice and experience, and who makes that particular work his study, than by persons who are only elected for a short period, who have no special qualifications for the duties of the office, and who may be succeeded by others who, perhaps adopting some different theory to their predecessors, may undo that which has been done, or cause injury by a neglect of duties, which having only undertaken for a limited period, they prefer leaving to their successor, rather than incur any odium by offending their neighbours, or by levying any extra expense necessary to maintain the work in efficiency.

CHAPTER V.

THE RIVER WELLAND AND DEEPING FEN.

The river Welland borders upon the county of Northampton on the one side, and the counties of Leicester, Rutland, and Lincoln on the other. It springs at Sibbertoft fields, in the county of Northampton, not far from the head of the Nene and the Avon, and flows thence by Harborough and Collyweston to Stamford, where it is increased by the river Gwash, and united they flow by Deeping and Crowland to Spalding, and thence to Boston Deeps, near the mouth of the Witham. The Gwash is about 20 miles in length. These rivers, springing in a comparatively high country, flow for a considerable distance through a low fenny district, the whole of which used to be overflowed by their waters. Hence an old saying, " Wasch and Wiland shall drown all Holland." The same authority tells us that the Welland is celebrated for its fish, for that " once in seven or eight years immense shoals of sticklebacks appear in the Welland below Spalding, and attempt coming up the river in a vast column. They are supposed to be the collected multitudes washed out of the fens by the floods of several years, and carried into some deep hole. When overcharged with numbers they are obliged to attempt a change of place; they move up the river in such quantities as to enable a man, who was employed in taking them, to earn for a considerable time, 4s. per day, by selling them at a halfpenny per bushel. They were used to manure land, and attempts have been made to get oil from them."

At Crowland is a triangular bridge which is described by Gough "As the greatest curiosity in Britain, if not in Europe." It consists of three piers or abutments, whence spring three arches, the groins of which are united in the centre. Three roads meet at the Crown; the ascent is very steep from each point, and the road is paved with stones. It is supposed to have been built about the year 941, but some authorities fix the date in Edward the First's reign. The river Welland, a branch of the Nene, and a stream called the Catwater used to flow under it,—the only water that now passes that way is covered in, and the roadway is under instead of over the bridge.

The Welland bears conspicuous mention in the annals of the ecclesiastical history of this country. Crowland Abbey, one of the earliest religious establishments founded in this country, being situated on its banks, monks became possessed of a great portion of the adjacent fens and marshes, which they endeavoured to re-claim by embanking and draining. The appearance of the country at the beginning of the 8th century is thus described:—"There is in the middle part of Britain a hideous fen of a huge bigness, which, beginning at the banks of the river Grante, extends itself from the south to the north in a very long tract, even to the sea: ofttimes clouded with moist and dark vapours, having within it divers islands and woods, as also crooked and winding rivers. When, therefore, that man of blessed memory, Guthlac, had found out the desert places of this vast wilderness, and by God's assistance had passed through them, he enquired of the borderers what they knew thereof, who, relating several things of its dreadfulness and solitude, there stood up one among them, called Tatwine, who affirmed that he knew a certain island, in the more remote and secret parts thereof, which many had attempted to inhabit, but could not for the strange and uncouth monsters and several terrors wherewith they were affrighted: whereupon St. Guthlac earnestly entreated that he would show him that place. Tatwine, therefore, yielding to the request of this holy man, taking a fisher's boat (Christ being his guide through the intricacies of this darksome fen) passed thereunto, it being called Crowland, and situate in the midst of the lake, but in respect of its desertness formerly known to very few, for no countryman, before that devout servant of Christ, S. Guthlac, could endure to dwell in it by reason that such apparitions of devils were so frequently seen there."

"Not long after, St. Guthlac being awoke in the night time, betwixt his hours of prayer, as he was accustomed, of a sudden he discerned his cell to be full of black troops of unclean spirits, which crept in under the door, as also at chinks and holes, and coming in both out of the sky and from the earth, filled the air as it were with dark clouds. In their looks they were cruel, and of form terrible, having great heads, long necks, lean faces, pale countenances, ill-favoured beards, rough ears, wrinkled foreheads, fierce eyes, stinking mouths, teeth like horses, spitting fire out of their throats, crooked jaws, broad lips, loud voices, burnt hair, great checks, high breasts, rugged thighs, bunched knees, bended legs, swollen ancles, preposterous feet, open mouths and hoarse cries; who with such mighty shrieks were heard to roar that they filled almost the whole distance from heaven with their bellowing noises; and by and by rushing into the house, first bound the holy man; then drew him out of his cell, and cast him over head and ears into the dirty fen; and having so done carried him through the most rough and troublesome parts thereof, drawing him amongst brambles and briers for the tearing of his limbs."
—*(Ingulph.)*

The reputation for piety acquired by St. Guthlac soon made Crowland famous, and after his death Ethelbald, King of Mercia, whose confessor he had been, determined to erect a monastery to his memory, and endowed it with the whole isle of Crowland, together with the adjacent fens lying on both sides of the river Welland. The ground on which the Monastery was built, being so moist and fenny as not of itself to bear a building of stone, a great number of piles were driven deep into the ground, and a quantity of firm hard earth, brought from a distance of nine miles, was thrown amongst them, and upon this foundation the building was erected.* A similar difficulty was overcome by the monks of Peterborough, who built a monastery in 655, and obtained a foundation by plunging into the marsh " stones so immense that eight yoke of oxen could scarcely draw one." (*Turner's History of the Anglo Saxons*). The bounty of the King was thus celebrated in poetry by an ancient monk :—

> " The Royal bounty here itself displays,
> And bids with mighty pains a temple raise.
> The soft, the slippery, the unsettled soil
> Had long disdained the busy workman's toil.
> No stone foundations suit this marshy land,
> But piles of oak in goodly order stand ;
> And boats, for nine long leagues, fetch filling land :
> The fickle soil cements to solid ground.
> The sacred pile on the firm base they found,
> And art and labour grace the work around.

It will be unnecessary further to pursue the History of the Abbey of Crowland, suffice it to say, though the Monks " had ample possessions in the fens yet they yielded not much profit, in regard that so great a quantity of them lay for the most part under water." The fens, however, served other purposes than that of profit, for in the many incursions of the Danes, they became the chiefest refuge of the Monks, their lives being secured by

---

* Ingulph's Chronicles of the Abbey of Crowland, Bohns Edition.
† A very interesting historical sketch of Crowland Abbey, written by the Rev. G. Perry, is published by the Society for promoting Christian Knowledge.

means of these spacious fens, in the reeds and thickets whereof they hid themselves to avoid the cruelties of this barbarous people, whilst the rest of their convent was murdered and their abbey burnt. The Monks had other enemies besides the Danes, continual efforts being made by the adjoining proprietors to wrest from them the lands given by the King, and again and again in successive reigns the Abbot had to appear before the King to get the charters confirmed. Thus Dugdale tells us "nothwithstanding that the lands and possessions of this abbey were, through the great bounty of several Kings and others, given thereto with divers ample privileges and immunities, and not only so, but with fearful curses pronounced by those pious persons against such as should violate any of their grants; nevertheless it appears that the inhabitants of Holand (bordering on the north side of Crowland), having drained their own marshes and converted them to good and fertile arable land, whereof each town had its proper proportion, wanting pasturage for their cattle, took advantage of a false rumour of the King's (Henry II.) death, and, bearing themselves not a little on their strength and wealth, thought that they might oppress the poor monks at Crowland without control." Accordingly they came down in a large body, pastured their cattle on the marshes of the abbot, cut and carried away his hay, and committed other depredations. He appealed to the King's justices, and for five years the contention was carried on, but at length the abbot prevailed and recovered possession of the marshes. In the reign of Henry III. the Abbot of Crowland being called upon by the King to make a road from his abbey towards Spalding, as far as a place called Brotherhouse, he pleaded that it would be a very difficult and expensive work, "because it was a fenny soil, and by reason of the lowness of the ground, in a moorish earth, it would be a difficult matter to make a causey fit and durable for passengers;

because it could not be made otherwise than upon the brink of the river Welland, where there was so much water in winter time that it covered the ground an ell and a half in depth, and in a tempestuous wind two ells, at which time the ground on the side of that river was often broken by bargemen and mariners, and by the force of the wind so torn away; so that in case a causey should be made there, it would in a short time be consumed and wasted away by the power of those winds, except it were raised very high and broad, and defended by some means against such dangers." The plea of the Abbot was admitted, but the men of Kesteven and Holland again urging on the King the necessity there was for a road, the Abbot at last undertook the construction, on condition that he might levy for seven years tolls sufficient to reimburse the cost and afterwards to maintain the road in good order.

In the same reign the town of Spalding was presented by the jurors before the justices, because they had neglected to scour out and repair the river Welland, where it passed through their jurisdiction, by reason of which neglect great damage had accrued to the King's liege people. The inhabitants of Spalding, being summoned by the Shiereeve to answer the charge, pleaded that the river then was and long had been an arm of the sea, wherein the tides did ebb and flow twice in 24 hours, and therefore that there was no obligation on them to repair it.

The river Welland was much injured by the loss of the back scour of the tidal waters, which at one time used to flow up and fill Bicker Haven. There is little known concerning the history of this arm of the sea, but that it occupied a considerable area may be gathered from the traces of its banks, which may be seen at the present time as far up as Bicker and near the turnpike-road, by which they are crossed between Sutterton and Gosberton. In the time of William the Conqueror it was still a receptacle for the tides, for the Abbot of Peterboro' is said to have had 16 salt pans at Donington, but the silting up must have taken place between this and Edward the Third's time, for in this reign the great dispute occurred between the Abbots of Swineshead and Peterborough as to whom the accreted land should belong, the area of Marsh more particularly involved in the law suit being 340 acres; the decision being given in favour of the ancient custom, " That all and singular Lords possessing any manors or lands upon the sea coast had usually silt and sand cast up to their lands by the tides." The Haven was also an outlet for a great quantity of fen and upland waters. By the old Skerth-drain it was connected with Kyme Eau, and by the Gillsyke with the lands bordering on the Upper Witham, and thus a great quantity of the land in the direction of Sleaford and Langrick would have the outlet for its waters by Bicker Haven.

About this time also a commission was appointed to inspect the river Glen, which adjoins Deeping Fen, and they decreed that it was not sufficiently wide " to admit of the proper discharge of the waters which it brought down from the higher part of the country, so that the fens on either side were drowned, and that it ought to be widened from Gutheram's Cote to the sea, so that at Surfleet it should be 20 feet wide;" and that the work ought to be done by the persons who owned the land abutting on the river. The same commission also presented that the great bridge, called Spalding Brigge, was then broken, and ought to be repaired at the charges of the whole town; and also that the Marsh banks, being then broken in divers places, should be repaired. The commission further ordained that all persons, as well rich as poor, should be liable to all mene works, as well for the repairs of the sewers as the banks; and that every man, having a messuage and 10 acres of land, should find one tumbril or cart, and those who had less, one able man of not less than 18 years of age; or instead of the cart and horse a money payment of fourpence, and instead of the man, of twopence per day. Numerous presentments of a similar kind were made from time to time against the Abbot of Crowland and others for not repairing the banks or properly scouring out the drains, and orders made thereupon. These banks and drains had originally been made by the Abbots of Crowland in their endeavours to reclaim the fens. Thus Abbot Egelvic so improved a portion of the marshes as to be able to plough and sow them with corn. Ingulphus's account is that " in dry years he tilled the fens in four places, and for three or four years had the increase of an hundred fold of what seed soever he sowed." The monastery being so enriched by these plentiful crops that the whole country thereabout was supplied therewith, and a multitude of poor people resorting thither for that respect made Crowland a large town. This state of prosperity did not continue, for in William the Conqueror's time they had no such inhabitants residing at Crowland, the only occupants of the adjacent fens being those of the tenants and their families, to whom the Abbot had let a great portion of the marshes and meadows, " no man delighting to inhabit here any longer than he was necessitated so to do ; insomuch as those who in time of war betook themselves hither for security (as great numbers of rich and poor from the neighbouring countries did) afterwards returned back to their particular houses, for without boats there was not then any access thereto, there being no path except up to the gate of the monastery." Abbot Egelvic was an enterprising man ; in addition to his banks and drains, and the ploughing up of the marshes, he also constructed a road from Deeping to Spalding, the foundation of which was made of wood covered with gravel, " a most costly work, but of extraordinary necessity."

In William the Conqueror's reign, one Richard De Rulos, Chamberlain to the King, being much given to good husbandry, such as tillage and the breeding of cattle, took in a great part of the common of Deeping Fen, and converted it into meadows and pasture. He also prevented the Welland from flooding his lands by a great bank, and on it he erected divers tenements and cottages, and made there a large town, whereunto he assigned gardens and arable fields, which town was called Deeping, the name originating from the constant floodings of these lands from the Welland, the meaning of the word being a deep meadow. By similar means he also made a village dedicated to St. James, now called St. James Deeping, and so by banking and draining he converted those low grounds, which before were only deep lakes and impassable fens, into fruitful fields and pastures, and the humid and moorish soil became a garden of pleasure.

Deeping Fen formed part of the great forest of Holland and Kesteven, the fen lands of which had been afforested by William Rufus, the bounds being afterwards extended by Henry the First as far as Market Deeping, and so it continued until the reign of Henry III., who disafforested all this fen " so that the lands, marshes, and turbaries were thenceforth quit of waste and regard."

The following particulars relating to Deeping Fen in the reign of Richard II. are given in Dugdale's history. "The marsh called Deeping Fen did extend itself from East Deeping to the middle of the bridge of Crowland, and the middle of the river of Welland, and thence to the messuage of Wm. Atte Townsend, of Spalding, and thence to a certain place called Dowe Hirne, thence to Goderham's Kote, thence to Estcote, and thence to Baston barre, thence to Langtoft-outgonge, and thence to East Deeping in length and breadth, and that the agistments of all cattle in the said marsh did then belong to the lord, and were worth annually XX*l.* ; and moreover that there was a certain profit of turfs, yearly digged therein, worth XX*l.* ; and likewise a profit of poundage, to be yearly twice taken of all cattle within the said marsh, viz., one time of horses and afterwards of cattle ; whereupon all cattle which have right of common there are delivered with payment of Greshyre, but of other cattle the lord hath Greshyre, which was worth XXl. per annum. Also that there was within the said marsh a certain profit of fishing, newly taken by reason of the overflowing of the waters on the north part toward Spalding, which was yearly worth VIIl., and that the other profits of fishing and fowling throughout the whole fen was worth Cs., and lastly that the fishing to the midst of the river of Welland to Crowland and thence to Spalding, was yearly worth Ls."

In this same (Richard II) reign a dispute occurred with the men residing in Kesteven as to the boundaries of the fens, and a commission was issued by the King. A perambulation having been made, ten crosses were erected to show the division. But within two years these were all thrown down and carried away by the Kesteven men, for which act sundry of them were hanged, some banished, and some fined in great sums, and command given for erecting new crosses of stone at the charge of these men of Kesteven. In several succeeding reigns Commissions were issued by the Crown to view the banks, ditches, and water courses, and also the floodgates and sluices, and to see that all necessary repairs were executed for maintaining the same in proper order.

In the beginning of the 16th century this part of the country is thus described by Camden in his history of England.

"Allow me, however, to stop awhile to describe the extraordinary situation and nature of this spot, so different from all others in England, and this so famous monastery (Crowland) lies among the deepest fens and waters stagnating off muddy lands, so shut in and environed as to be inaccessible on all sides except the north and east, and that only by narrow causeys. Its situation, if we may compare small things with great, is not unlike that of Venice, consisting of three streets, divided by canals of water, planted with willows, and built on piles driven into the bottom of the fen, and joined by a triangular bridge of admirable workmanship, under which, the inhabitants report, is a pit of immense depth, dug to receive the confluence of waters. Beyond this bridge, where, as the poet says, 'the soil cements to solid ground,' antiently stood the monastery so famous, in a much narrower space all round which, except where the town stands, it is so moory that you may run a pole into the ground to the depth of 30 feet, and nothing is to be seen on every side but beds of rushes, and near the church a grove of alders. It is, notwithstanding, full of inhabitants, who keep their cattle at a good distance from the town, and go to milk them in little boats, called skerries, which will hold but two persons; but their chief profit arises from the catching of fish and wild fowl, which they do in such quantities that in the month of August they drive 3000 ducks into one net, and call their pools their fields. No corn grows within five miles of them. Higher up that same river lies Spalding, surrounded on all sides with rivulets and canals, an handsomer town than one would expect in this tract among stagnated waters. From hence to Deeping, a town ten miles off, the meaning of which is deep meadow, for the plain below it extending many miles is the deepest of all this fenny country, and the receptacle of many waters; and, which is very extraordinary, much below the bed of the river Glen, which runs by from the west, confined within its own banks."

In Queen Elizabeth's reign an Act was passed for making the Welland navigable, from Stamford to the Sea. Drakard in his history of Stamford, says: "That this Act was obtained on the application of the aldermen, burgesses, and commonalty of Stamford, stating that their town, which had formerly been inhabited by many opulent merchants, whose wealth had been increased by the navigation of the river Welland, and its connection with Boston, Lynn, and other parts, was then gone to great ruin from the prejudice done to the navigation, by the erection of mills between Deeping and Stamford, and the consequent diversions of the stream from its ancient course." And at a general session of the Commissioners of Sewers, holden at Stamford, on the 23rd of August and the 10th of September, in the 17th year of King James the First, by that Act of Parliament it was enacted and decreed that it should be lawful for the Corporation of Stamford to make a river, of such breadth and depth as they should think fit, for the passage of boats and barges, from the north side of the river Welland, from the east end of the town of Stamford, and Hudd's Mill, across the river called Newstead River or the Wash, and thence through Affington, Tallington, West Deeping, Market Deeping, and past Market Deeping Corn Mill, to rejoin the ancient course of the river, and thence in the course before stated unto the outfall to sea, at Boston Deeps. The Corporation were enabled to make such locks, sluices, and other works as were necessary for the navigation, the expense of which undertaking was then estimated at £2,000. The Commissioners of Sewers also ordained, as this work was undertaken at the expense of the Corporation and their friends, that the aldermen, and burgesses, and their successors should receive, for all boats passing through each lock, such a competent consideration as should be fit and convenient. This order was confirmed by King James the First, who fixed the tonnage at the sum of threepence; and also, granted to the Corporation the fishery of the new river. The tolls arising from the navigation were leased by the Corporation of Stamford at a very nominal rent; first to one, Daniel Wigmore, and subsequently to others.

The length of the cut from Hudd's Mill below Stamford to the lock, at East Deeping, was nine miles and a half, and on this length twelve locks were erected, which were made of a capacity to receive vessels of seven feet beam. Vessels of greater burden than fifteen tons could not navigate the cut; and before the construction of railways the goods, consisting chiefly of coal and timber, were usually taken up to Stamford in gangs of four lighters, of from seven to fourteen tons burden. The voyage from the Scalp, at the mouth of the river Witham, where the ships lay to discharge their cargoes, through Spalding to Stamford was about 50 miles, and was performed in three or four days.

In Queen Elizabeth's reign a petition was presented to the Queen by the inhabitants of Deeping and the other towns having right of common in the fens, viz., Deeping, Spalding, Pinchbeck, Thurlby, Bourn, and Crowland, setting out the lost condition of these fens, owing to the decay of the banks of the Welland and the Glen, and the condition of the sewers and water courses, and that by properly draining the same these fens might be greatly improved ; and praying the Queen to direct a Commission of Sewers to make enquiry and undertake such works as they should deem necessary for their recovery, and recommending a Mr. Thos. Lovell as the undertaker for such works, he having acquired a considerable knowledge of draining in foreign parts.

In compliance with the prayer of the memorialists, a Commission of Sewers was issued, which sat a Bourn, and also at Market Deeping. After inquiry, they granted to Lovell a concession of the right to drain these fens, on condition that the same should be done solely at his own expense within a period of five years. As recompense, he was to have a third part of the reclaimed land, but only on condition that he should maintain the works in a state of efficiency, and perfect the drainage of the fens so that they should be firm and pasturable both in summer and winter. Lovell at once commenced operations, and expended the whole of his fortune, about £12,000, but owing to the opposition of the fenmen, who broke down his banks and otherwise destroyed his works, the attempt was unsuccessful. A few years later the Commissioners for the drainage of the great Bedford Level, sitting at Wisbech, laid a tax of thirty shillings an acre on Deeping Fen for the purposes of reclamation, which not being paid, the Commissioners of Sewers made certain proposals to King James the First, who directed Sir Clement Edmonds to visit the fens, and report to him as to their condition, and also as to the state of the Welland. The Commissioners found the river so bad that they were forced to carry their boats three or four miles between Spalding and Fosdyke for want of a current to carry them down the channel, the water then being only six inches deep at a distance of two miles below Spalding. The King, having heard Sir Clement's report, in answer to the petition, signified his pleasure by the Lord Bishop of London to let them know that they might proceed to make a decree for the further and more perfect draining of the fen, and thereby to award as well from his Majesty, being lord of the soil, as from the former adventurers and others interested therein such proportion of land as might sufficiently bear the charge of the work; and, because his Majesty intended to see the whole of the Great Bedford Level prosecuted accordingly to his first princely design (it being for the country's good and his own service) in a manner that would most conduce to the public and general advantage of the whole fens, he was further pleased to declare himself the sole adventurer for the drainage of Deeping Fen. The King was unable to carry out his royal intentions, and matters remained in abeyance until the 17th year of Charles the First, when a fresh Commission being appointed they found that the Earl of Exeter was the owner of one-third of the Fens, by contract made with Thomas Lovell, the former adventurer, but that he had not carried out the terms of the original contract, the fens still remaining drowned; and they therefore granted one-half of the land to Sir William Ayloff and Sir Anthony Thomas, the great contractors of those days, in consideration of their undertaking the drainage. They, in partnership with other adventurers, at once set about the "exsiccation" of the fen; and for this purpose widened and deepened the Welland from Spalding to the sea, and made it navigable: they also cleaned out and enlarged the drain which had been cut by Lovell, which passed under the Welland by a sunken tunnel near Cowbit. Another drain, called the Staker, 20 feet in width, was cut parallel with the Glen to relieve that river. Another drain, called Hill's drain, was also cut, which discharged into the Welland at Spalding, where was erected a great sluice. The Vernatt's drain, running from Pode Hole past Surfleet to the sea, was also made at this time. The banks on both sides of the Welland, made by the former adventurers, were also strengthened and completed. These banks are placed at a great distance apart, in some places as much as a mile, leaving a large area of land, which forms a reservoir for the waters in times of heavy floods, and relieves the pressure on the banks of the river. These spaces or "washes," which used formerly to grow only flags and reed grass, now are very valuable either for fodder or the pasturage they afford to great numbers of cattle which are turned on them in the summer months. In winter they are under water; and if the temperature falls sufficiently low become frozen, and form a splendid skating ground. Cowbit wash has long been celebrated for its skaters, and people have come from all parts of the country to join in the matches that are held there.

By the works above enumerated the land was so well drained that in summer the whole fen yielded great quantities of grass and hay, and would have been made winter ground in a short time, but that the country people, taking advantage of the confusion throughout the whole kingdom, which ensued soon after the convention of the long Parliament, possessed themselves thereof; so that the banks and sewers, being neglected by the adventurers, it became again overflowed, and so remained nearly 100 years.

In 1650 Sir Cornelius Vermuyden in carrying out the works for the drainage of the Bedford Level, in order to protect the "North Level" from the waters of the Welland, constructed a bank, extending from Peakirk to Crowland, and thence to Brotherhouse, where it unites with the Holland Bank. This bank was made seventy feet broad at the bottom and eight feet high, and an excellent road is now maintained on its top, forming a direct communication between Peakirk and Spalding.

The next attempt to drain these Fens appears to have been made in 1729, by Captain Perry, an engineer who had been engaged on works in the Thames, who erected windmills for working wheels for lifting the water out of Deeping Fen into the Vernatt's drain. These mills do not appear to have been very successful, the fen being reported subsequently to be almost in a lost state.

Stone, in his review of the survey of the agriculture of Lincolnshire, remarks: "The drainage of Deeping fen is chiefly effected by three wind engines, above Spalding, that lift the Deeping fen water into the Welland, the bed of which is higher than the land to be drained, assisted by a side cut called the West Load, which falls into the Welland just below Spalding, and which district, in violent floods, in a calm when the engines cannot work, is reduced to a most deplorable condition, more especially when the banks of the Welland give way, or overflow, as happened in 1798."

The sluice at the end of the Glen was erected some few years after this, for an inscription on it bears date 1739, and states that it " was erected and built by order of the honourable adventurers of Deeping Fen, according to the model and direction of Messrs. Smith and Grundy."

In the year 1794 an Act was obtained (34 Geo. III. c. 102) for improving the outfall of the river Welland, for the better drainage of the fen lands, and for improving the navigation of the river, by means of a new cut to be made from a place called the Reservoir, in the parish of Surfleet, near where the Vernatt's drain and the Glen river discharge into the Welland, to be carried thence through the enclosed and open salt marshes into Wyberton Roads. For the purpose of carrying out the Act, a body was constituted called the Welland Commissioners, and the money was raised by a tax on the lands, distributed as follows :— Deeping fen and common were to pay eighteen pence an acre ; lands in Cowbit and Crowland washes six pence an acre ; Spalding and Pinchbeck old inclosures, between the Glen and Westlode, six pence ; Pinchbeck, north of the Glen, twopence ; lands in Surfleet, Gosberton, Sutterton, Quadring, Algarkirk and Fosdyke, draining by Risegate Eau, or by the five-towns tunnel, twopence an acre. The design was partially carried out, the contemplated new cut extending only as far as Fosdyke bridge. Seven years afterwards, in 1801, an Act was obtained for draining, dividing, allotting, and enclosing Deeping, Langtoft, Baston, Spalding, Pinchbeck, and Cowbit commons, and also for draining Croyland common, otherwise called Goggushland. Under the powers of this Act (41 Geo. III. c. 128) several large arterial drains were either newly cut, or the old ones (made by Lovell and others) altered and enlarged, which brought the whole of the waters off the fen and discharged them into the Vernatt's drain at Podehole. The principal drains constructed at this time were the South Drove drain, $8\frac{3}{4}$ miles in length ; the North Drove drain, $5\frac{3}{4}$ miles ; the Cross drain and the Counter drain, $6\frac{3}{4}$ miles. The total distance of the outfall, at the confluence of the Witham and the Welland, from Podehole about 15 miles, or 18 miles from the lowest lands in the fen, and the fall from the surface of the lowest lands at low watermark was about 15 feet.

Fosdyke Bridge was built in the year 1812 by a private company, an Act having been obtained for the purpose.

In 1824, an amended Act (51 Geo. III. cap. 71) having been obtained, the Welland Commission was reconstituted, and was made to consist of thirteen trustees, one of whom was to be elected by the Corporation of Stamford, and one by the owners of the old enclosed lands in Spalding and Pinchbeck. The trustees were to be elected every three years, and their special duty was "the maintenance, support, and improvement of the new cut from the Reservoir to Fosdyke, and the drainage and navigation thereby." They were relieved from the liability entailed on them by the former Act from extending the new channel lower down than Fosdyke Bridge, and were authorised to carry out works for the removal of shoals in the Welland from and below the staunch fixed across the river above Spalding, and through the town, and for training the waters through Fosdyke Marsh. They were also authorised, for navigation purposes, to place draw doors across the mouth of the river Glen at the request of the Deeping Fen Adventurers and the Dykereeves of Gosberton, Surfleet, and Pinchbeck. To assist in paying for these improvements, the tax of one shilling for Deeping Fen, and such parts of the late commons as had been sold by the Inclosure Commissioners, and sixpence per acre on the lands between the Glen and the Westlode was continued; the allotments of the commons, the lands north of the Glen, and those draining by Risegate Eau, and the five-towns sluice being exonerated from further payment; and the trustees were further empowered to demand tonnage on all vessels using the new channel of the Welland, the tolls being fixed at a maximum of 2d. per ton on coals, 4d. per last on oats, 4d for the half last of wheat, and 4d. per ton on general goods, and other rates in proportion. This Act was again amended (in 1837) by the 1 Vict., cap. 113, which, after reciting that the river had become deteriorated, and the taxes sanctioned by former Acts were not sufficient, gives power to raise them according to a fixed schedule. The principal dues were by this Act 3d per ton on all ships and boats, 3d. per quarter on wheat, other corn $1\frac{1}{2}$d., coals 6d. per ton. The money raised was to be applied to the improvement of the river from Spalding to Clayhole, by training and embanking it. Power was also given to erect quays and wharves, to levy wharfage rates, to employ pilots, and hire and maintain a pilot sloop, and appoint a harbour master.

Spalding is part of the Port of Boston, and up to the year 1842 all vessels navigating the Welland had paid tonnage and lastage dues to the trustees of that port; but by the Act 5 Vict., cap. iv., in consideration of the Welland Trustees paying to the Boston Harbour Trustees the sum of £5000, being part of a debt then due to the Exchequer Loan Commissioners on the security of the tolls and dues, and also paying one-third of the annual expenses to be incurred by the Boston Harbour Commissioners in maintaining the buoys, beacons, and sea marks of the port; the said trust was to give up all claim to dues on vessels navigating the Welland, and the Welland Trustees were authorised to collect a tonnage rate of sixpence, and lastage rate of one penny on wheat, and one halfpenny on other corn. Under the same Act, and also another passed in the same year, the Boston Harbour Trust and the Welland Trust were empowered severally to execute any works for the improvement of the navigation of their rivers up to the point of confluence; and below that jointly to execute any works for the improvement of the outfall of the said waters into Clayhole.

The taxes and tolls authorised to be levied by these Acts not proving sufficient to maintain these works, in the Session of 1867 another Act was obtained, giving powers to the Trustees to bring into taxation again the lands which from 1794 until the act of 1824 had been taxed; and also other lands which had hitherto used the river as the outfall for its waters, without contributing to the expense of its maintenance; for from the preamble of this Act, it appears that out of 85,000 acres of land draining by the Welland, only 24,000 paid taxes, producing £535 per annum;

and that the dues from vessels, which in 1846 had exceeded £6000, had gradually diminished to £998 in 1865. At this time there were charges on the trust to the amount of £6000 due on mortgage, and the sum of £1000 in addition had been borrowed of the treasurer, on the personal security of the Commissioners, to carry out works of emergency. From this it would appear that the revenues at the disposal of the Commissioners had become most seriously diminished, owing to the decline of the navigation, arising no doubt from the alteration in the method of transit for all articles of produce and consumption, and chiefly of corn and coal, by the formation of railways. The only communication the interior of the fens had with other parts of the country, previous to railways, was by means of boats navigating the arterial drains and the great fen rivers; but the greater certainty and convenience of the railway system has to a great extent superseded the canals, and Spalding, with all towns similarly situated, has suffered accordingly. The land has benefitted to a very considerable degree and increased in value, owing to the railways, and can therefore easily afford a small additional burden for the maintenance of the outfall drainage, on the preservation of which its whole prosperity depends.

Having thus named the various legislative enactments which have been made with respect to this district, there remains now only briefly to notice the engineering operations that have been carried out under the powers of the various Acts, and the present state and prospects of the river. Commencing with this century, the first engineers who were engaged in this district are Messrs. Rennie, Maxwell, Hare, and Jessop, whose reports chiefly relate to the interior drainage of Deeping Fen, and the improvement of the Vernatt's Drain. In the year 1812 a report was made by Mr. Bevan, on the improvement of the navigation and drainage of the river Welland. He describes the river as being greatly improved by the new cut made from the Reservoir to Fosdyke, but that below that point the river had a very winding channel, obstructed by sands and shoals. To remedy this, he proposed that a new cut should be excavated from Fosdyke Fen, through the marshes, to the Witham opposite Hobhole, and that a sluice should be erected at the end of this cut. The expense of this and other improvements was estimated at £150,000.

In 1815, Mr. Thomas Pear made a report to the effect that the drainage was in a very unsatisfactory condition, the water often standing six feet on the cill of the old Vernatt's sluice, which was the outlet for the drainage of Deeping Fen, including an area of 30,000 acres, which were drained by means of fifty wind engines. This outlet was over-ridden by the waters of the Welland and the Glen. The cause of this was the defective state of the outfall below Fosdyke bridge; neap tides, which rose 15 feet at the junction of the rivers, never reaching Spalding, a distance of 15 miles. He proposed as a remedy, a new cut two miles in length, commencing at a point near the Holbeach and Whaplode sluice, and about two miles below Fosdyke inn, to be made through the embanked lands and open salt marshes, and ending with an outfall near Holbeach middle sluice; the channel to be fifty feet wide, and five feet above the low-water mark in the south channel, with a rise of one foot per mile. He also proposed the erection of a lock or new sluice, a little above the Reservoir, for the purpose of keeping up a navigable head of water in dry seasons, and to be so contrived as to admit the free influx of the tides, and at the same time to be clear for the outflowing of land water; and a similar pen sluice for the river Glen; the estimated cost of the improvements he put at £50,000.

In the year 1818, Mr. John Rennie made a report to the proprietors of lands in Deeping Fen on the improvement of the outfall of the Vernatt's drain. The result of his survey of the district was that he found the whole of Deeping Fen "almost in a lost state." At that time the sluice at Pode-hole, where the Vernatt's drain commences, had three openings of 10 feet each, giving a water way of 30 feet. The Vernatt's sluice, the outlet of the drain, had two openings with the same width of water way. This sluice, some years later (in 1842), was blown up, the water having forced its way under the foundations, and was replaced in 1857 with a new structure, built from the designs of the late Mr. Lewin, the cill being placed several feet lower than the old one. The foundation-stone was laid by Sir John Trollope. Mr. Rennie approved the scheme already proposed for making a new cut from Fosdyke to the Witham, but as a modification of that plan, he proposed that a new cut should be made from the Vernatt's sluice, to take the Deeping Fen waters only, passing under the Glen by an aqueduct, and running along the north bank of the Welland to Fosdyke; then along the enclosed lands for half a mile, across the sea bank, and along the open marshes to the Witham at Hob-hole, with a sluice at the end. The length of this channel would be $8\frac{1}{4}$ miles, the total distance from the Cross Drove drain in Deeping Fen, to the outfall, being $23\frac{3}{4}$ miles, and ordinary low water mark at that time, standing at three feet three inches on Hob-hole cill, which was 17 feet below the surface of the land in the fen, allowing the water to stand two feet under the surface of the land, and giving a fall throughout the whole length of the new channel of six inches per mile. This cut would also take the waters discharging from the lands draining by the Gosberton Five Towns and Kirton Outfalls, amounting together to 18,000 acres. The estimated cost of this work was £123,650. In recommending this plan, Mr. Rennie was no doubt influenced by the principle which he always so strongly advocated, of concentrating all the waters possible into one tidal outfall; and, regarded as a matter of principle, and as part of a whole scheme, of which the Witham was the outfall, there is no doubt he was correct; but for the plan to have been successful it would have been necessary that the outfall of this river should have been dealt with in a very different manner from that which subsequent experience has shown to be the case. Mr. Rennie based his calculations on the fact that low water mark at Hob-hole would be maintained at the same level as he then found it; but the utter neglect of this part of the river Witham, combined with improvements in the upper reaches, has resulted in a gradual raising of the low water mark of from three to four feet; low water at Hob-hole cill now constantly standing at seven and eight feet.

Mr. Rennie's plan not being adopted, a report was obtained from Mr. Thomas Pear, who recommended the application of steam power for the drainage of this fen, which at this time was very imperfectly accomplished by wind engines, being sometimes wholly under water. This recommendation was endorsed by Mr. Bevan, who, in a report dated March 1st, 1823, advises the erection of two engines at Pode-hole, and the deepening of the drains. Being thus advised, the Deeping Fen Trustees obtained the necessary powers, and in the year 1824 the engines were erected. These are two condensing beam engines of 80 and 60 horse power, working two scoop wheels, the larger of which is 28 feet wide, with five feet float boards. The average immersion is about two feet ten inches, and the head of water against which the engines have to work is sometimes as much as six feet. Owing to the subsidence of the land—the improved cultivation and working of which had the effect of depressing the surface of the fen as much as two feet—the wheels have recently had to be lowered. The large wheel revolves at the rate of four miles an hour, and the two wheels, when at full work, can discharge

300 tons of water per minute. The total quantity of land drained by the engines is 25,000 acres, and the number of days the engines run varies from 50 to 100, according to the season. The working of these engines at first was not so satisfactory as was anticipated, and Mr. W. S. Mylne, C.E., a very eminent authority on the subject, was called in to report on them. In his report, dated July 16th, 1830, he condemns the erection of two engines in one place, the drains not being able to supply them without lowering the level of the water near the engines too low for advantage to the land. He further advised the lowering of the wheels and the deepening and improving of the interior drains. Whatever the first effect may have been, there is no doubt that the ultimate effect has been the reclamation of this fen, which before their erection, had been in a half cultivated condition, and subsequently has grown excellent crops of wheat and other produce, and the value of the land nearly doubled.*

No steps having been taken to carry out the recommendations for the improvement of the outfall, it gradually became worse and worse, till in the year 1835 it was reported that at low water, in dry seasons, there were only a few inches of water at Fosdyke. Vessels drawing three feet of water could not float except at the top of spring tides, and vessels drawing six feet could not depend on floating at springs, and no vessel, except barges, could reach Spalding at all. In fact the state of the river had become so bad, that the Commissioners were compelled to take active measures, or see the whole drainage of the district ruined. Mr. Jas. Walker, C.E., was therefore consulted, and in an able and

---

* Arthur Young, in his survey of Lincolnshire, speaking of Deeping Fen, says:—
" Twenty years ago the land sold for about three pounds an acre; some was then let at seven and eight shillings an acre; and a great deal was in such a state that nobody would rent it, now it is in general worth twenty shilling an acre, and sells at twenty pounds. Ten thousand acres of it are taxable under commissioners, and pay up to twenty shillings, but as low as two shillings; the average is about four shillings, including poor rate and all tithes free."

detailed report, bearing date November 7th, 1835, he sets out the works he considers desirable for the improvement of the outfall. These consisted in training the river, in the first instance, as far as Holbeach middle sluice, a distance of nearly three miles, and ultimately to Clayhole. The area of the uninclosed space, or estuary, below Fosdyke bridge he found to be 5000 acres, 4000 of which were available for reclamation. The estimated cost of the fascine training for the two miles seventy four chains was £13,000, and the advantage to be gained—a very considerable lowering of the bed of the river, and the more rapid discharge of the water. Mr. Walker's report having been approved, powers were obtained, as already mentioned, to increase the tolls, and the money having been borrowed of the Exchequer Loan Commissioners, the work was commenced by Mr. Beasley.

The plan adopted by Mr. Walker for training the river was first proposed to him by Mr. Beasley, and was found to be so simple and inexpensive, as compared with other methods, and at the same time so effective, that it has since been used in all similar works in the estuary. It consists of barrier walls, or banks made of thorn faggots about six feet long and three feet girt, which are laid in the water in courses varying in width in proportion to the depth, and as each course, which is weighted with clay, sinks, others are laid on till the bank is raised to about half tide level. The branches of the thorns interlace one with another, and the silt brought up by the tides rapidly deposits amongst and at the back of this fascine work, and thus a solid embankment is formed, of sufficient strength and tenacity to withstand the strongest tidal current.

From a subsequent report of Mr. Walker's, it appears that in October, 1838, the new channel had been successfully formed with fascine work for one and a half mile below Fosdyke bridge, the cost of this portion being £7026. The good result was immediate and most satisfactory, for vessels drawing eight feet of water could get along the new channel to Fosdyke with greater certainty than those of three feet could before, the water consequently being lowered nine feet. Mr. Walker concludes this report by saying that his original design extended to carrying the channel four miles below the bridge, but that this ought not to be the limit of the work, and adds, " where nature is at hand to do so much, the direction should be extended quite to the Witham."

The fascine work was extended about another mile after this, with still further advantage, for in 1845 it is reported that the effect of the fascine work had been to lower the river about seven feet from Fosdyke Bridge downwards. The recommendation of Mr. Walker for its continuance has not been attended to; but on the contrary, owing to a scarcity of money, arising from causes already alluded to, the work which was then perfected was neglected, in consequence of which the tides gradually worked behind the fascine work, and the whole was in danger of being swept away. But after a considerable loss had been incurred, the Trustees and some of the Proprietors interested, met at Spalding on the 27th of August, 1866, and convinced of the urgency of the case, by the report of their able Superintendent, Mr. Kingston, determined to borrow sufficient money, on their own personal liability, to put the fascine work in sufficient repair to prevent further damage until they could apply to Parliament for increased powers of taxation. In 1867 an Act was obtained, as already mentioned, and the funds placed at their disposal by the additional lands brought into taxation by the Act of last Session, will enable the Trustees to maintain the present works; but it must be a matter of regret that a more comprehensive scheme for extending the training to the junction of the Witham was not brought forward. It has been stated by no less an authority than the late Mr. Pear, who was most intimately acquainted with the district, that in his opinion " there is no part of these fens but what is susceptible of the most complete natural drainage without the aid of engines or other appliances;" and if this be the case there is no doubt that a natural drainage is far preferable to an artificial one. A comprehensive scheme, which would embrace the training, by fascine work, of the two rivers Witham and Welland to one common outfall, while rendering available the reclamation of several thousand acres of now useless sands, would at the same time improve most materially the navigation and the drainage, and add to the prosperity of the country; and even if it be found that, owing to the subsidence of the soil, Mr. Pear's theory is no longer correct, yet the head of water could be so lowered as to render unnecessary the use of the engines except in extreme floods, affecting a large annual saving in coals and working expenses. It is no new experiment: the plan has been tried, and found to be successful at a moderate cost. Wherever training has been carried out, an immediate and palpable benefit has ensued; and no money which has been laid out on drainage has ever brought a better return than that which was expended on the main outfalls. Unless these are preserved all interior drainage must prove defective.

CHAPTER VI.

THE ORIGIN AND CONSTITUTION OF THE COURT OF SEWERS.

Until the reign of Henry the VIII., the watercourses and sea banks of the country may be said to have been without any special protection, and great loss was frequently incurred by the eruption of the tides through neglected banks, and by the flooding of the country, owing to obstructions in the rivers caused either by accumulation of deposit, or by weirs and mill dams placed across them by persons for their own profit and advantage. There was of course a remedy at common law, but the difficulty and uncertainty of obtaining redress led generally to an appeal to the King, for we are told "that our ancient monarchs were much interested in preserving their dominions from the ravages of the sea, and that their subjects were as careful to second these designs by keeping up a system of drainage. Accordingly, on the one hand, it is to be found in our legal history, that it was not only the custom of the Kings of England, but their duty also, to save and defend the realm against the sea, as well as against enemies, so that it should neither be drowned nor wasted; and on the other, that to stop the water channels which were made from time to time for public or private convenience, was a grievous offence punishable by action or indictment, according to the nature of the wrong; that it was held that the King's subjects ought by the common law to have their passage through the realm by bridges and highways in safety, so that if the sea walls were broken, or the sewers and gutters not secured, that the fresh waters might have their direct course, the King was empowered to grant a commission to enquire into and hear and the district, that in his opinion " there is no part of these fens but what is susceptible of the most complete natural drainage without the aid of engines or other appliances;" and if this be the case there is no doubt that a natural drainage is far preferable to an artificial one. A comprehensive scheme, which would embrace the training, by fascine work, of the two rivers Witham and Welland to one common outfall, while rendering available the reclamation of several thousand acres of now useless sands, would at the same time improve most materially the navigation and the drainage, and add to the prosperity of the country; and even if it be found that, owing to the subsidence of the soil, Mr. Pear's theory is no longer correct, yet the head of water could be so lowered as to render unnecessary the use of the engines except in extreme floods, affecting a large annual saving in coals and working expenses. It is no new experiment: the plan has been tried, and found to be successful at a moderate cost. Wherever training has been carried out, an immediate and palpable benefit has ensued; and no money which has been laid out on drainage has ever brought a better return than that which was expended on the main outfalls. Unless these are preserved all interior drainage must prove defective.

CHAPTER VI.

THE ORIGIN AND CONSTITUTION OF THE COURT OF SEWERS.

Until the reign of Henry the VIII., the watercourses and sea banks of the country may be said to have been without any special protection, and great loss was frequently incurred by the eruption of the tides through neglected banks, and by the flooding of the country, owing to obstructions in the rivers caused either by accumulation of deposit, or by weirs and mill dams placed across them by persons for their own profit and advantage. There was of course a remedy at common law, but the difficulty and uncertainty of obtaining redress led generally to an appeal to the King, for we are told " that our ancient monarchs were much interested in preserving their dominions from the ravages of the sea, and that their subjects were as careful to second these designs by keeping up a system of drainage. Accordingly, on the one hand, it is to be found in our legal history, that it was not only the custom of the Kings of England, but their duty also, to save and defend the realm against the sea, as well as against enemies, so that it should neither be drowned nor wasted; and on the other, that to stop the water channels which were made from time to time for public or private convenience, was a grievous offence punishable by action or indictment, according to the nature of the wrong; that it was held that the King's subjects ought by the common law to have their passage through the realm by bridges and highways in safety, so that if the sea walls were broken, or the sewers and gutters not secured, that the fresh waters might have their direct course, the King was empowered to grant a commission to enquire into and hear and determine the defaults."—(*Callis.*) Again, Fitzherbert says "that these commissions were granted when the sea walls were broken, or when the sewers and gutters were in need of repairs, so that the fresh waters could not have their courses; and that the commissions in question issued, because the King was bound of right so to keep his kingdom against the sea, as that it were not drowned, or wasted, and also to provide that his subjects should pass through the kingdom with safety."—(*Woolrych on the Law of Sewers.*)

The commission, thus issued by the King, consisted of two or more persons holding either a judicial position in the kingdom or of considerable standing, who were directed to hear all complaints, and had power to levy fines and make orders for the necessary works to be done for repairing and maintaining the sea banks, and cleansing and keeping open the sewers. The commissions were issued by virtue of the King's prerogative at common law, and the first parliamentary recognition of sewers and sea defences was in the days of Magna Charta, by which it was provided that no town, nor freeman, should be distrained to make bridges or banks, but such as of old time and of right had been accustomed to do so, by which it appears that the maintaining of the sea defences had been considered a special grievance by those who had been distrained for their repairs.

Commissions continued to be issued by the Crown in virtue of the King's prerogative until the reign of Henry VI., when it was enacted by Parliament that, considering "the great damage and losses which have happened by the great inundation of waters in divers parts of the realm—Lincolnshire being particularly mentioned,—and that much greater damage is likely to ensue if remedy be not speedily provided, that during the years next ensuing several commissions of sewers shall be made to divers persons by the Chancellor of England for the time being," who were to enquire of annoyances of defaulters to repair the sea banks, and make such orders as they deemed necessary, with power to fine and distrain those who refused to obey them.

These commissions were renewed by succeeding Parliaments until the sixth year of Henry the VIII. reign, when they were declared to endure for ever, and the Chancellor was invested with perpetual authority to grant such commissions wherever need should require. This Act was incorporated with another, passed in the 23rd year of the same reign, in which all the former enactments were contained; and although some alterations and additions were made in the reigns of Edward the VI. and Queen Elizabeth, yet the 23, Henry VIII., cap., 5, still continues to be considered the chief structure on which the powers and duties of commissions of Sewers have been reared. In the reign of William the IV. several alterations were made in the original enactment, to adapt its working to modern times; but the principle of its original constitution remained unaltered.

The purpose for which the court was created was the preservation of marsh and low lands, and the maintenance of the sea banks and other defences, and the removal of impediments and obstructions made in the streams or sewers by the erection of mills, mill-dams, weirs, gates, &c., and they were to have survey over " all walls, fences, ditches, banks, gutters, gates, sewers, callies, ponds, bridges, rivers, streams, water courses, &c."

The word sewer appears in modern times to have a much more restricted, if not different meaning attached to it from that originally intended. The common acceptation of the word now is invariably associated with the disposal of the refuse water from dwelling houses and towns; whereas formerly, it was applied to the protection of land from inundations, whether by the erection of banks, or by confining the rivers and streams in their proper channels. Authorities differ as to the derivation of the word, the opinion of the learned Sergeant Callis, the great authority on the Law of Sewers, being that it was the diminutive of a river. Others tracing it to a corruption of the word "issue;" or seoir, to fit, and eau water; or to sea and mere. According to one of these surmises, a sewer might be defined a wall or dam opposed to the inroads of the ocean; or if the last be adopted, a fresh water trench supported by banks on either side for the purpose of carrying water into the sea. This last meaning is the one still attached to the word in the seas and marshlands, but beyond those parts the word now is used solely to denote those structural arrangements for the cleansing of towns and thickly populated places, which are deemed so necessary to the health and comfort of the inhabitants.

The word "Gowt," "Gote," or "Goat" which has received frequent mention throughout these pages, and which also may be considered as peculiar to fens and marshes, is used to express a certain construction in connexion with drainage, as for instance Anton's Gowt, Slippery Gowt. The word is derived from the Saxon, and is defined by Callis to be "an engine erected and built with percullesses and doors of timber, stone, or brick." Their use is said by the same authority to be twofold: the first to cause fresh water which has descended on low grounds to be let out through them into some creek of the sea; and the second, to return back salt water direct, which during some great floods of the sea may have flowed in upon the land.

Romney Marsh, a tract of land in the county of Kent, seems to possess the privilege of having first drawn up any definite rules for the guidance of commissions of sewers, and which formed a a precedent for the custom of all other fens and marshes. Nearly all the commissions, and even the statute of Henry VIII., directing that the laws and customs of the commissioners are to be made after the laws and customs of Romney Marsh." Thus also at the building of the Grand Sluice, by May Hake, in Henry the Seventh's reign, assessment was made to raise the money, and the same was ordered to be levied according to the laws of Romney Marsh. Whence also were obtained a bailiff, juratts, and levellers. These laws were attributed to Sir Henry de Bathe, a judge in the reign of Henry the III.; and Lord Coke observed, " that not only those parts of Kent, but all England receive light and direction from those laws."

The Court of Sewers, as now constituted, consists of persons holding freehold property in any part of the county to which the commission belongs, and who have qualified themselves by taking the necessary oaths.

Persons qualified must by the Act of William the IV. be in possession of property in the county in which they shall act as Commissioners, of the yearly value of £100; or of lands held for a term of years of the clear yearly value of £200; or be heirs apparent to a person possessed of freehold property of the clear value of £200 : or the agent of qualified persons or bodies corporate holding freehold property. Every Commissioner before he can act must take an oath in the form set out in the statute of Henry the VIII. to perform his duties faithfully, and also as to his proper qualification.

It will be observed that the word " Court " is used, and the proceedings are not purely ministerial, but are judicial, and consequently that there is a " Court ;" and as Mr. Callis observes, " Their Court is one of record, and an eminent Court of record." And so Lord Coke, when writing of courts, enumerates among them " The Court of Commissioners of Sewers."

The commission lasts for ten years, at the end of which time, or on the demise of the reigning sovereign, a fresh commission is issued out of chancery; but the proceedings of the old commission, after being once recorded in the rolls of the Court, remain in force after its expiration. The Court may meet at such times as they think fit, but ten days notice of the intended meeting must be given by advertisement in a newspaper of the County. Six members form a court, and at each meeting those present elect their chairman.

The court has power to direct the sheriff to summon a jury " to enquire of or concerning all or any of the matter and things authorised and directed to be enquired into, under any of the Acts and Laws of Sewers of old time accustomed, and to administer oaths to such jury."

The first duty of a new commission is to summon a jury, who are to make a presentment as to the person liable to maintain and repair, or to contribute towards the repair and maintenance of all defences, banks, and other works under their jurisdiction; and the verdict of such jury once had holds good during the whole time of the existence of the commission.

The Commissioners have power to levy rates, as occasion may require, for every distinct level, valley, or district ; and to appoint such surveyors, collectors, treasurers, and other officers for such district. This is the wording of the Act, but the ordinary course of proceeding is for each parish to appoint two officers, called in this county 'Dykereeves,'—to collect the rates and maintain the banks and sewers,—and these appointments and all their proceedings, are subject to the approval of the court. The dykereeves present their accounts to the vestry of the parish, at Easter. Surveyors are appointed by the court itself, who have the general supervision of the works, and when defects exist, their duty is to make a presentment to the court, who then order the dikereeves of the parishes in which the work is situated, at once to amend and repair the same, and levy rates for its payment.

The obligation to maintain the sea banks originally was on those whose lands adjoined the sea, and this was called the custom of frontagers, and which duty can only be put off by showing that some other persons are bound by prescription or otherwise. Again, this obligation attaches to some lands by the nature of their tenure, although such lands may not be near the sea ; but the difficulty of dealing with individual liabilities, when the safety of a whole level depends on immediate action, has principally thrown the obligation of repairs by custom on the whole township. But numerous instances still remain, where individual proprietors are liable ; and in case such persons do not maintain the particular banks, sluices, or sewers to which they are liable, after seven days' notice from the surveyor or dikereeve, the court may order the same to be done, and the expenses can be recovered by distress.

This leads to a consideration with respect to the ownership of the sea banks. Mr. Callis says that "the ownership of a bank of the sea belongs to him whose grounds are next adjoining, according to the principle adopted concerning highways." This ownership, of course, is only a limited one. The freehold belongs to the frontager or other person entitled thereto, and all advantages and privileges, as the herbage of the bank, &c., are his; but the Court of Sewers has complete control over the bank, and the owner cannot do any act to injure the safety or stability of the same. The custom with respect to the herbage of the banks is various—there can be no doubt that originally, where the frontager was liable to repair, this herbage naturally belonged to him ;—but when this obligation of repair was shifted on the township or parish, the privileges attaching, in most cases, went with it, as a means partly of defraying the expenses of maintenance of the banks. In many parishes the grass on the banks is regularly let, and the proceeds carried to the credit of the parish fund ; in others they have been treated as common or waste land and sold under inclosure awards—while again in other parishes the frontagers still continue to claim the right—and no doubt the custom in each case has operated so long as to have become a right.

As bearing on this subject it will not be out of place to refer to the great dispute which took place in Edward the Third's reign, between the Abbots of Peterborough and Swineshead, as to the proprietorship of the marsh land on the exterior of the banks which accreted by the deposition of the alluvium washed up by the tides, a process which was evidently going on rapidly in those days. The various commissions, arbitrations, and trials concerning this suit were spread over a period of 25 years, and it was only finally settled by an appeal to Parliament.

The contention appears to have been as to the ownership of certain marshes in Gosberton (part of Bicker Haven) which had accreted, and which lay in front of the manor of the Abbot of Swineshead, on which ground he claimed it. The Abbot of Peterborough on the other hand set up a claim because, although it lay in front of the Abbot of Swineshead's Manor, it was separated from it by a creek, the accretion of the land having gradually extended from the Manor of Peterborough in a lateral direction, so as to overlap the land of the adjoining proprietor. The following is the account given by Dugdale of the commencement of the proceeding:—" Memorandum : That in the year of our Lord MCCCXLII., 16 Edward III., the Abbot of Swinesheved and Sir Nicholas de Ry, Knight, did implead the Abbot of Peterborough for CCCXL. acres of marsh, with the appurtenances, in Gosberchirche, viz., the Abbot of Swinesheved for CC. and Sir Nicholas for CXL., by two writs. And the first day of the Assizes at Lincolne was on Wednesday, being the morrow after the feast of St. Peter ad Vincula ; at which time there came thither Gilbert de Stanford, then Celerer to the convent, John de Achirche, bailiff of the said Abbot's Mannors ; together with Sir

John Wilughby, Lord of Eresby; Sir John de Kirketon, and Sir Saier de Rochford, knights; John de Multon, parson of Skirbek, as also divers others of the said Abbots Counsel. And because the defence of this trial seemed difficult and costly to the Abbot, in regard that his adversaries had privately and subtilly made the whole country against him, especially the Wapentake of Kirketon, he submitted to an amicable treaty of peace, on the day preceding the assize, the place of their meeting being in the chapter house of Lincolne: at which treaty, in the presence of Sir Nicholas de Cantilupe (who was the principal mediator betwixt them, as a friend to both sides) and other knights and friends, above specified, the said Abbot of Swynesheved and Sir Nicholas de Ry did set forth their claim in that marsh; affirming that it did belong to them by right, by the custom of the country; because that it was increased and grown to their own ancient marshes by addition of sand which the sea had by its flowings cast up; insomuch as by that means coming to be firm land, they said that they ought to enjoy it, as far as Salten Ee; and in regard that the said Abbot of Peterborough had possessed himself thereof, contrary to right, and against the said custom, they had brought the assize of *novel disseisin* in form aforesaid.

"Whereunto the Counsel for the Abbot of Peterborough answered that the custom of this province of Holand, so stated by the plaintiffs, ought thus to be understoood and qualified, viz., that when, by such addition of any silt or sand, there should happen an increase of land, and, by the seas leaving thereof, become firm ground, it ought to belong unto him to whose firm and solid ground it first joined itself, without any respect whether it grew directly to it, or at one side. And they further said that the before specified marsh did originally join itself to the ancient marsh of the said Abbot of Peterborough, whereof that monastery had been seised time beyond memory, as it appeared by Domesday Book, where it is recorded that the Abbot of Peterborough had XVI. salt pans in Donington; moreover in the Charter of King Richard the First, there were confirmed to the said Abbot three carucates of land, with the salt pans and pastures, and all their appurtenances, in Holand: so that the said soil increasing little by little ought not to belong to the Abbot of Swinesheved and Sir Nicholas, according to the custom of the country; because that a certain part of Salten Ee, which was not then dry land, did lye betwixt the old marsh belonging to the said Abbot of Swinesheved and Sir Nicholas, and the marsh whereof they pretended to be disseised: which part of Salten Ee could not at all be drained; because that the fresh waters used to run through that place from the parts of Kesteven to the sea."

It will be unnecessary to follow the case through all its various stages, the final settlement was made by six arbitrators who awarded that the Abbot of Peterborough was to pay a certain sum of money to the others, and they in return were to give up all their right to the marsh. "And as to the future increase of ground, which might happen to either party, that it should be enjoyed by him to whose land it did lie most contiguous." And this was confirmed by the Parliament which sat in the 17th year of King Edward the Third's reign. But the question was again raised and was not finally settled till the 41st year of King Edward's reign, " when was that memorable verdict touching the customs of the country, that the lords of manors adjoining to the sea should enjoy the land which is raised by silt and sand, which the tides do cast up."

The Court of Sewers has power besides the maintenance of old and existing defences, to make and construct new works, when it is necessary for the more effectually defending and securing any lands within the jurisdiction of the court, against the irruption or overflowing of the sea, or for draining and carrying off the superfluous waters, but such new works cannot be made without the consent in writing of the owners or occupiers respectively of three fourths part at least of the lands lying within the valley, level, or district proposed to be charged with the costs and expenses of making and erecting such new works. When such consent is obtained the Court can borrow money for the execution of the works, to be repaid with interest in a period not exceeding fourteen years.

Under the Land Drainage Act of 1861, Commissions of Sewers may, with the approval of the Inclosure Commissioners, be issued for districts where they have not formerly existed if it can be shown that the state of the drainage is such as to require some controlling body to superintend the outfalls ; but as the Act also gives the option between a Commission of Sewers or an Elective Drainage District, the latter method has been generally adopted in those places where the provisions of the Act have been applied.

Thus it will be seen that the Court of Sewers is not only an ancient but a very important body of Commissioners, with responsible duties and extensive powers. They can summon juries, administer oaths, lay rates, levy fines, and issue distresses. Many of their acts are judicial, and can only be set aside by appeals to the higher courts. Before the existence of the Witham, Black Sluice, and other Drainage Commissioners, the whole of the sewers and drainage in this neighbourhood were under the control and management of the Court of Sewers, and even now there are few parishes which do not depend on the sewers, gowts, and sluices of the Court of Sewers for their drainage. The whole level of the fens, being under high water mark, would be covered with water at high spring tides but for the sea banks erected by the Romans, and now under the jurisdiction of this Court; and although perhaps not perfect in its constitution, the immunity of the country from any serious damage by floods in late years is a proof that its functions are as necessary, as well performed.*

---

* The contents of this chapter are an addition to the papers on the Fens which appeared in the *Stamford Mercury*, but the greater part appeared in the *Lincolnshire Herald* of Oct., 1866.

CHAPTER VII.

BOSTON HARBOUR AND HAVEN.

The port of Boston consists of all that portion of the river Witham and its estuary from the town to the sea, over which the Corporation holds control under the charter granted by Queen Elizabeth. By this charter they are enabled to exercise Admiralty jurisdiction "within the borough and port and also the roads and the deeps, commonly called the Norman Deeps, and over all streams and washes extending to Wainfleet Haven, and to a place called Pullye Heads, and to another place called Dog's Head in the Pot, and to the uttermost limits of the flowing and ebbing of the waters aforesaid and every of them, and adjoining to the sea and floods and streams of the borders and confines of the county of Norfolk;" and also to take tolls and dues of all vessels entering the port, the proceeds of which were to be applied towards keeping the channel properly buoyed out.

The positions of the buoys and beacons as first placed under this charter were as follows :—The first, nearest to Boston, at Westward Hurn; the second at South Beacon; the third at Scalp Hurn; the fourth between Scalp Hurn and Elbow Beacon; the fifth, the Elbow Beacon, at Stone Hawe; the sixth, South Clay Beacon; the seventh, the North Clay; the eighth, midway between the North and High Hurn; the ninth at High Hurn; the tenth on the Main between Boston and Benington; the eleventh and last, on the Long Sand. These beacons were fixed for the first time in the year 1580, and a survey of them was made in the month of August by the Mayor, Aldermen, and sundry Master Mariners—a practice which has been continued annually up to the present time.

In the year 1796 an Act was obtained for the management of the pilotage, and the regulation of the rates; the conduct of the same being committed to a trust consisting of the Corporation and certain qualified Master Mariners and Merchants of the town.

The dues which the Corporation was entitled to receive under their old charter proved insufficient to maintain the harbour in a proper state of repair, and in consequence the quays went to decay and the river became much neglected; their powers also being ill defined, encroachments were made on the river to the detriment both of the drainage and navigation. To remedy this state of things the Corporation obtained an Act of Parliament in the year 1812. This Act repealed the old tolls, and in their place granted certain wharfage dues (according to a schedule) on all goods landed or shipped from any wharf or quay between the Grand Sluice and Maud Foster, the tonnage dues being fixed at sixpence for British and ninepence for foreign vessels. A lastage duty of one penny per quarter on wheat and one half-penny on other grain was also imposed on all corn whatsoever put on board or landed out of any ship within the limits of the port. On the security of these dues the Corporation were authorised to raise a sum of £20,000 to build new quays and wharves, and to improve the river by widening and deepening and contracting the same. The new wall built along the eastern side of the river, from the south end of the Pack House quay to the bridge, and thence to the Fish-market, and the large warehouse on Packhouse quay, called the "London warehouse," were part of the improvements effected. About this time, also, a considerable improvement was made by straightening the upper part of the river by a new channel cut from the Grand Sluice to the Iron Bridge, the cost of which was £8550, the work being contracted for by Messrs. Williamson and Woodward.

Notwithstanding the works carried out under this Act, the navigation continued to be very much impeded by the state of the river below Maud Foster sluice. Several efforts had been made to induce the Drainage Commissioners to join with the Corporation in straightening and improving this portion of the river. Mr. Rennie had advised them to contribute liberally towards the cost of the work, and reported that a considerable saving could be effected in the drainage of the east and west fens by bringing the whole of the waters to Maud Foster instead of making a new cut where the Hobhole drain now is, but that to enable this to be done the river must first be improved.

The Harbour Commissioners were prepared to contribute one-half the cost of the work; and at a meeting held at Boston, December 9th, 1800, at which were present several merchants, shipowners, and traders, it was " resolved that to promote the improvement of Boston Haven there shall be levied on all vessels entering inward and clearing outward at the port of Boston a duty of fourpence per ton; which duty there is reason to believe will be equal to the interest of about one half the capital sum which the said improvement will require according to the estimate of Mr. Rennie." The Drainage Commissioners declining to join with the Corporation on the ground that their scheme did not go far enough, inasmuch as it did not include the improvement of the outfall below Hobhole, the river was allowed to remain in its imperfect condition until 1825, when Sir John Rennie having been called in to advise, an Act was obtained in 1827 by which the Corporation were empowered to borrow a further sum of £20,000, and to carry out the works recommended by their engineer. These consisted of the straightening of the river by means of a new cut, 800 yards in length, through Burton's Marsh, thus cutting off the great bend at Wyberton roads, and shortening the distance to deep water one mile and a half. The contract for this work was undertaken by Messrs. Joliffe and Banks for the sum of £24,000, and finally completed in the year 1838, at a total cost for land and works of £27,262.

The remainder of Sir John Rennie's plan, embracing the straightening of the river from Skirbeck church to join this new cut, was not commenced till the year 1841, when Capt. Beasley undertook to train the channel, which was continually shifting between these two points, by fascine work, and to excavate where necessary, so as to make the river as nearly straight as possible. This work he successfully accomplished at a cost (including land) of £11,627. In the following year Mr. Beasley completed a fascine barrier on the west side of the river, from nearly opposite Maud Foster Sluice to the end of Slippery Gowt Marsh, the length of the same being about one mile, at a cost of £2775; and the water being thus confined in one channel, the land on either side gradually accreted, till it became level with the top of the fascine work, and rose to such a height as only to be covered with water at the top of the spring tides. The land so formed has been embanked within the last three years by Mr. Black and the Corporation, and where once the waters meandered about through shifting sands, the plough now is driven, and crops of corn and other produce are raised.

Another considerable piece of training was the diversion of the waters from their circular course round Blue Anchor Bight Marsh to a straight line, by the fascine work carried out by the late Mr. Robt. Reynolds, and the same result has followed on the inside of this work, as already mentioned as taking place higher up the river. The sands and Marsh are now good agricultural land, having been embanked two years since. The amount expended by the Corporation in improving the channel of the river is as follows :—

	£	s.	d.
1825.—Cutting new channel for the river from the Grand Sluice to the Iron Bridge	3550	0	0
1828 to 1833.—Cutting a new channel through Burton's Marsh, diverting the old channel	27,262	0	0
1841.—Cutting a channel through Corporation Marsh, and making a fascine barrier on the eastern side of the river from Maud Foster to Corporation Point	11,627	0	0
1842.—Fascine barrier on the west side of the river from Rush Point to the south end of Slippery Gowt Marsh	2,775	0	0
1823 to 1859.—Sundry small contracts for extension of fascine work	7,555	0	0
Fifteen years' expenditure in repairing and heightening the fascine work, and general maintenance of the river	5,250	0	0
	£58,019	0	0

The shortening and straightening the river to deep water has been greatly serviceable to both navigation and drainage : the river is now maintained in as great a state of efficiency as practicable by the Corporation. The whole of the navigable channels are buoyed out, lights are placed when the tides serve in the dark, during the six winter months, at certain fixed points from Elbow buoy to the town by which vessels can steer their course. A pilot boat is always afloat in the lower part of the harbour, and an efficient staff of pilots maintained.

It has been stated that the Corporation under their ancient charter were entitled to collect dues from all vessels entering the port, which right was confirmed to them by the Act of 1812 ; but in the year 1842 an Act was obtained by which the dues on vessels navigating the Welland were transferred to the trustees of that river, and in consideration they were to pay to the Harbour Commissioners one-third of the cost of maintaining the buoys, beacons, and sea marks. By the same Act it was enacted that the Harbour Trustees should have the power to execute any works for the improvement of the river as far as the point of confluence of the Witham and the Welland, but beyond this all works are to be done jointly and only with the consent of both trusts.

The number of vessels frequenting the port of Boston has of late years very considerably diminished. The following statistics of the tonnage and lastage and the dues will show the state of trade of the port at different periods :—

Year.	Tonnage of Goods.	Quarters of Grain.	Dues.	
			£ s. d.	
1800	52,698	—		
1805	62,980	201,898		
1810	86,256	356,040		⎧ The greatest
1811	—	360,699		⎨ number of qrs.
1815	66,786	246,160		⎩ ever recorded.
1820	—	247,535	2216 10 10	1818 to 1833
1830	—	149,709	2406 7 9	[books burnt.
1835	69,386	—		
1840	61,354	141,759	3300 1 2	
1845	73,413	—		
1848	94,060	—		G.N.Ry. opened.
1849	56,800	—		
1850	55,110	114,399	1866 5 0	
1855	38,031	57,910	1160 6 0	
1860	40,147	65,547	1297 7 7	
1861	46,962	93,485	1522 2 6	[reduced to 3d.
1862	43,220	72,066	805 3 2	Tonnage dues
1863	41,687	132,725	981 16 7	Last on wheat
1864	42,439	113,491	768 15 11	[reduced to ½d.
1865	38,860	102,004	739 9 9	
1866	38,014	103,256	691 4 3	
1867	40,124	127,329	766 18 0	

The above returns are for the twelve months ending the 11th of October in each year. The dues at present levied are threepence per ton on all goods, and one halfpenny per quarter on *all* grain shipped at the port. The Commissioners have power to raise these dues to sixpence per ton on goods and one penny per quarter on wheat.

The decrease is in a great measure owing to the construction of the Great Northern Railway, the loop line of which through Boston was opened in the year 1848. Before this time a very considerable trade was carried on by means of the Witham and other navigable canals with the interior of the country. Previous to 1848 the river was the only means of conveyance for the export of the corn brought to Boston from the large agricultural district by which it is surrounded, and for the import of the coals and other produce for consumption by the inhabitants of the fens, which were brought by sea to Boston and carried thence by boat and barge up the canals and drains to the fens. On the opening of the railway a fresh means of communication was provided, and a considerable amount of traffic diverted to it from the river. A very large trade in inland coals was also carried on by the Witham, the quantity which passed down through the Grand Sluice gradually increasing from the beginning of this century from about 12,000 chaldrons to upwards of 30,000 in 1830. The duty being taken off sea coal in this year caused the amount to diminish to about 13,000 chaldrons. From the opening of the railway in 1848 a steady decrease again took place, and the quantity now passing down the Witham is merely nominal compared to what it used to be.

Several schemes have been promulgated from time to time for providing the port of Boston with better accommodation for its shipping. The most noticeable was a plan brought out by Mr. Staniland in the year 1845, at the time the Great Northern Railway was in progress. The company was organised under the name of the Boston Dock Company, with a capital of £200,000, its professed object being the "further improvement of the Haven and Outfall and the construction of Wet Docks." The scheme was very strongly supported, the Mayor of Boston and two-thirds of the Corporation being on the Provisional Committee, also seven magistrates of the borough, and several commissioners of the river Witham and Black Sluice, and a long array of landowners and merchants. The prospectus stated "That the port of Boston has for ages been the natural point of access to the ocean for a very extensive and exceedingly fertile tract of country. In early ages Boston ranked amongst the principal seaports of the

Island: in late years, however, partly owing to neglect and partly to other causes, the outfall has become bad and the navigation difficult." This state of affairs the company proposed to remedy by their scheme, and they considered the time a particularly opportune one, as the construction of the various railways then in progress would bring the port in connection with the whole of the Midland Counties. This scheme, so promising in appearance, proceeded no further than the formation of the company. The scarcity of money at the time, and other difficulties, caused the promoters to abandon it.

The last attempt to improve the Port was made by the promoters of the Boston and Freiston Shore Railway, who proposed to construct a line from the Great Northern Railway, in Skirbeck Quarter, to Clayhole, opposite Freiston Shore, and there to construct a large pier and breakwater, by the side of which vessels of large size might lay afloat at all states of the tide. The bill having passed through the preliminary stages in the House of Commons was withdrawn, owing to its not being adequately supported; and its sister measure, got up by the same promoters for the reclamation of the marshes adjacent to their proposed railway, which became law, has not hitherto been acted on.

Reference has already been made to the lands that were gained by the improvements which were made in the river in the years 1833 and 1841. The largest tract, containing about three hundred acres, was sold by the Harbour Trustees to the late Mr. Black, in the year 1863, for the sum of £10,000, which enabled them to pay off the whole of the money remaining due on mortgage, which had been borrowed to effect the improvements in the river; and and also to reclaim the two other marshes, containing together about 160 acres. These marshes were enclosed from the tidal waters by two embankments a mile and a half in length, the waters from the parish of Wyberton and the adjoining land being discharged through a sluice built for that purpose in the Slippery Gowt embankment. The contract for the embankments was carried out by Mr. George Hackford, from the plans and under the direction of the author. A house and farmstead has also been erected on the smaller enclosure, and during the last two seasons the land has yielded large crops of wheat and other produce.

The income of the Harbour Trustees is derived from the rent of these lands and other property, and from the dues, and on an average of the last three years has been as follows:—

	£	s.	d.
Tonnage dues	738	0	0
Wharfage dues	265	0	0
Rent of land and warehouses	365	0	0
Total	£1368	0	0

The average ordinary expenditure for the same period has been:—

	£	s.	d.
Maintenance of buoys and beacons, less one third paid by Welland Trustees	418	0	0
Repairs of buildings, wharfs, stages, &c.	100	0	0
Rates, taxes, and insurance	41	0	0
Gas for lighting harbour	57	0	0
Repairs and maintenance of river banks, fascine work, &c.	100	0	0
Salaries and office expenses	220	0	0
Total	£936	0	0

From this it will be seen that the Trust has, on their ordinary expenditure, an excess of income over disbursements, and they have also power to increase the dues, which may be fairly calculated to raise the surplus to upwards of £800 a year, amply sufficient to cover the interest and re-payment of principal on a sum of money sufficient to complete the training of the river a distance of two miles below the present fascine work, or nearly to Elbow buoy.

The various schemes which have been suggested for the

improvement of this part of the estuary will be fully treated in the next chapter; and it will be found that the amounts required in each case are far too large to be entertained by any one Trust connected with the Witham, and have ever proved a complete drawback to their completion; * but the plan proposed by the author of this work, and more fully treated in a former publication, is one that appears to him to afford all the improvement that is necessary for the purposes of navigation; while it can be carried out at a cost, as shown, that comes within the means of the Trustees of the Harbour.

---

* Remarks on the State of the Outfall of the River Witham, with suggestions for its improvement, 1867.

BOSTON ADMIRALTY SEAL.

CHAPTER VIII.

THE ESTUARY, THE OUTFALL OF THE RIVERS WITHAM AND WELLAND, WITH AN ACCOUNT OF THE VARIOUS SCHEMES WHICH HAVE BEEN SUGGESTED FOR ITS IMPROVEMENT.

The Estuary of the Witham and Welland is also the receptacle of the waters of the Nene and Ouse; it forms a large indent or bay, lying between the coasts of Lincolnshire and Norfolk, and is about three hundred square miles in extent: it has considerably decreased in size, about one hundred square miles of land having been reclaimed since the original embankments of the Romans. Mr. Chapman, in his "Facts and Remarks," gives it as his opinion "that there probably was a time, subsequent to the last great wreck of nature, when this estuary was nearly free from sand-banks; and that the vast accretions of soil in and upon its margin owe their origin, in no small degree, to the alluvion of a large tract of land which the sea has carried away between Skegness and Saltfleet, and also from the Norfolk coast." Whether this were the case or not the bay is now full of large beds of sand, rising to a height of ten or twelve feet above low water; and although many of these sands retain the same position which they have done for a very long period, others are continually shifting, from the effects of the tide and wind, and altering the many channels through which the waters find their way to the sea.

That these sands have been formed by the alluvion of the lands from the neighbouring shores is highly probable. The coast north of Boston Deeps has been washed away to a considerable extent. At Sutton the sea is said to have advanced more than seven miles, and at Mablethorpe the roots and trunks of many trees, and large stones (the supposed ruins of a church) are visible at low water a mile from the shore. The name of Skegnesse, the termination "nesse" meaning a nose, or projection, would denote that at one time it projected beyond the line of coast into the sea; and Leland informs us "that this place was formerly a great haven town having a castle."

The set of the tides on this coast running from north to south, and passing by and not directly through this estuary, naturally forms an eddy, and causes the soil and other matters brought with the tides to be deposited. Subsequent tides carry this deposit higher up the bay, and in course of time form large shoals and sand beds, this process being still further assisted by the mud and other deposit brought down the drains and rivers in times of flood. That the sand is gradually but slowly encroaching on the space now occupied by waters is an undisputed fact, and one for which there can be no cause for regret, provided only reasonable care be bestowed in training the channels of the river, as these sands may in time become reclaimable land.

The Witham enters this estuary at the end of the new cut at Hobhole, and pursues a devious course in a southerly direction through shifting sands to the point known as the "Elbow," where it is met by the Welland. The distance from Hobhole to the Elbow by the present course is about three miles, the channel varying in width from a quarter of a mile to a mile. On its east side is a hard bed of clay, called the Scalp, and on the west it is bounded by salt marshes lately enclosed. The course of the river through this channel varies with the strength of the ebb and flood tides; in summer, when there is no fresh water issuing from the river, the flood tides prevail, and keep the channel to the east along the hard bed of clay composing the Scalp; in winter, when heavy freshes are running down the river, the current opposite

Hobhole is driven from its natural course by a barrier erected for the purpose of sending the waters into Hobhole Sluice; it then strikes against the embankment of the enclosed marsh, runs for a short distance along the scalp, from which it is reflected towards the west, gradually working its way by washing down the bed of sand, six to seven feet in height, thrown up in the summer months, till at the end of a wet season the channel will have altered its lateral course from three-quarters of a mile to one mile. At times it will vary as much as 80 to 100 feet in one tide. At the end of the scalp the Witham is joined by the Welland, which impinges on the waters of the Witham at a right angle, and diverts it from its natural course, causing the stream to turn in a north-easterly direction, and forming a long elbow; the two streams combined continue together to deep water at Clayhole. Below this the streams again divide, the north channel running in a line parallel with the coast for about fifteen miles, past Freiston, Butterwick, Benington, Leverton, Leake, Wrangle, Friskney, and Skegness, where it passes out into the German Ocean; it is divided from the other or south channel throughout its whole length by high beds of sand, the depth of water varying from about one and a half to six fathoms, and decreasing towards its exit at the Outer Knock buoy, where there is a bar with only a depth of nine feet of water at low water spring tides. The width of the channel alters in nearly the same proportion, from a quarter of a mile to a mile and a quarter, but is contracted again at its outlet to about a quarter of a mile.

The other channel, leaving the north-easterly direction a little below Clayhole, flows down what is termed "the Maccaroni," making an acute angle with its former course; and after running in this direction for a mile and three-quarters it doubles back up the Gat Channel into Lynn Well. The depth of water in the Maccaroni is from one to two fathoms, in the "Gat" it increases to six fathoms, and continues deep water all through Lynn Well, the bed of the estuary in places being as much as 18 fathoms below the surface of the water. The length of the north course is about 20 miles, and by the south, by vessels going in the same direction, is about seven miles longer. Through these two channels the greater part of the waters of the Witham and Welland have to flow before reaching the ocean.

The present course of the waters of the Witham and Welland round the Elbow to Clayhole is not the ancient or natural course, but is caused by the two streams meeting at nearly right angles. The alterations which have been made during the last century in the Witham have been the means of withdrawing the back scour of the tidal waters, which used to have a free run for 20 miles or more up the river, and of the large reservoirs formed by the windings of the river and the creeks and sands which are now embanked marshes. The abstraction of water has considerably altered the strength of the Witham stream; and the Welland, having still the free run of the tides, has to a certain extent prevailed over the larger river and driven it from its natural course. On reference to ancient plans and charts, and from information obtained from old sailors, it appears that the channel originally, after leaving the Scalp, continued with an easy curve in a south-easterly direction past the Herring Sand, through the Maccaroni, into Lynn Well. This is termed the old south channel, and was the regular course for vessels navigating the Deeps. It is still partially open, and is used by fishing-smacks and other vessels of light draught; and through it a part of the waters of the Welland find their way to the sea.

From this description of the estuary it will be obvious that the great obstruction of the free current of the downfall waters is the great mass of shifting sands with which they have to contend. The channels continually varying as the sands are affected by the winds, the tides, or the floods, the waters exhaust their strength in forcing their way through them, and the power which should be employed in deepening and scouring is lost by the waters being spread over a wide surface instead of being concentrated in a single channel of uniform width. The better to illustrate this it may be mentioned that an ordinary tide will take three hours to reach Hobhole Sluice after it is flood in Clayhole, a distance by the present winding course of four and a half miles; and as soon as it reaches the confined channel of the Witham, its speed increases to such an extent that it flows over the same distance of four and a half miles and reaches the Grand Sluice in less than one hour. The difference of level between Hobhole and Clayhole, in the year 1799, was three feet three inches, in a course of four miles, or nine and one-third inches per mile. In 1822 the course had lengthened to five and a half miles, and the waters were so much held up by the filling of the river with sands that the fall had increased to five feet two inches. The present rate of inclination in the surface of the water from Hobhole to Clayhole is about eight feet, or at the rate of twenty-one and one-third inches per mile. Spring tides rise 25 feet at Clayhole, and flow from four to five hours; neap tides rise about 16 feet. The semi-diurnal period, during which the state of the ebb will allow the discharge of the fen waters, is from five to six hours, dependent, of course, in a great measure, on the state of the haven. Spring tides ebb out at Clayhole about four feet lower than neap tides. The rise of the tide and the depth to which the ebb flows out is greatly affected by the wind. A strong north-west wind causes the tide to flow higher and longer; a south-east wind, on the contrary, causing a bad tide. The winds will make a difference of from three to six feet in the height of the tides.

A singular circumstance has long been noticed respecting certain tides in this estuary, called " bird tides." These occur annually about Midsummer, and are almost always much lower than others throughout the year; leaving the green marshes on the borders of the estuary free from any visitation of the tidal waters, although covered by spring tides at all other seasons. The occurrence of these low tides about the time when the numerous sea and land birds that frequent these Marshes are hatching their eggs, thus giving them time to perfect that operation without the destructive intervention of the salt water, has caused the country people to say that "the tides are lower at that season in order that the birds may hatch and raise their young!" (*Thompson.*)

Boston Deeps is often used as a harbour of refuge for vessels during north-east gales. When nearly the whole of the coals were carried from the north by colliers, these vessels used during storms, to take refuge in the Estuary; and it is stated by persons residing near the coast, that they have seen from 300 to 400 ships lying within a space of three miles off the coast between Freiston and Wrangle, and this was considered one of the safest anchorages in England during north-east gales.

The Wash affords a very valuable fishing ground. The fish principally taken are soles, shrimps, herrings, sprats, mussels, oysters, and cockles; smelts are occasionally found, and cod is caught in the deep water outside the Estuary. From 40 to 50 smacks are employed by the Boston fishermen, and as many by Lynn. These boats during the summer months are engaged in fishing for soles, shrimps, &c., and for the other nine months in gathering mussels. There are eight principal mussel scalps extending along the bay, within the Boston boundary, covering an area of from six to eight square miles; and within the Lynn boundary there are ten scalps, of from eight to ten miles in extent. There are also beds on the Hunstanton coast, on the property of Mr. L'Estrange. All the mussels required for bait for the fishermen engaged in the deep sea line fisheries on the Northern coasts, are taken from these places and sent by railway to the various fishing ports. Thousands of tons are also sent to the manufacturing towns for food. The yield for nine months in the year has been estimated at from 80 to 140 tons of mussels for food, and from 80 to 120 tons for bait. In busy seasons, from £700 to £800 worth of mussels have been sent away in a week. The sum paid to the Railway Company for carriage from Boston alone, has been stated for one year at upwards of £3000.

In 1859 the Corporation of Boston, in conjunction with Lynn, drew up and issued regulations for the protection of the fishery, and took steps to enforce their rules ; but it was ascertained that although their charters enabled them to issue regulations, there was no provision made for enforcing penalties, and consequently the orders of the bailiff were disregarded. The fishery is again carried on in the most destructive manner, and is being completely ruined.

From the evidence given before the fisheries' commission, which sat at Boston in 1863, it appears that previous to the appointment of the water bailiff by the corporation in 1859, the brood of mussels on the various sands in the deeps was almost exhausted. The fishermen raked them up large and small together, the riddlings being used for manure. Whole boat-loads of the young brood were carried to the Norfolk coast to put on the land. During the time the regulations of the Corporation were obeyed, these practices were stopped, and in two years' time the beds were again covered with mussels ; but as soon as it was found that the magistrates had no power to impose penalties, the destructive manner of fishing was resumed, and in 1868 it was reported that some of the richest beds had become completely exhausted, and the fishermen suffering from want of employment ; the supply of bait had ceased, causing very great distress to the population of the fishing towns and villages in the North. The same consequence has ensued with the oysters, shrimps, and soles. So serious was the matter felt to be, that the Northern fishermen sent a deputation to the Corporations of Boston and Lynn, praying them to take some steps to stop this sad waste; this was seconded by a memorial to the Corporation of Boston, signed by 132 smack owners and fishermen belonging to the port, and in consequence the Corporation has applied to the Board of Trade for further powers to regulate the fisheries under the oyster and mussel fisheries Act of the present session.

Having thus given a general description of the estuary, there will now follow a detailed account of the various schemes which have from time to time been brought forward for training the outfall of the rivers through a fixed channel and so facilitating their discharge, increasing the draught of water, and generally improving the drainage and navigation; and also for reclaiming the vast tracts of Marsh lands on the coast of the estuary.

The first scheme for the improvement of the outfall was that proposed by Mr. Nathaniel Kinderley in the year 1751. Adverting to the fact that even at that time the outfall waters of the Nene, the Ouse, the Witham, and the Welland, the four rivers which disembogue into the estuary, were seriously impeded by the shifting sands which were being continually washed about by the tides, he says, " But what do we propose to do with these pernicious sands ? Do we think to remove them ? No, certainly that would be quite an impracticable scheme; but though we can't remove them, we may certainly desert them, *and if we don't we may be assured that the sea in time will desert us.*"   *
    *   *   He therefore proposed to bring the Nene into the Ouze by a new cut through Marsh land, these rivers when united to be carried to the sea under Wooton and Wolverton through the Marshes, and to discharge themselves

into the deeps by Snettisham. The Welland was to be taken by a new channel inland from about Fosdyke, in the direction of Wyberton, to the Witham, near Skirbeck Quarter, and the two rivers united to continue in a straight course through the country to some convenient place over against Wrangle or Friskney. The result of this he considered would be the entire silting up of the estuary and the gaining of 100,000 acres, the whole of which would become good land in the course of 50 years: "A new habitable country 15 miles long and from 8 to 10 in breadth." Across this new formed country he proposed that a road should be made connecting Lynn and Boston. The cost was estimated at £150,000, and Mr. Kindersley naively compares this amount with that being spent on the old Westminster Bridge, £400,000, and asks: "what is the convenience of this bridge compared to the gaining to the nation of a whole county?"

Of all the schemes which have ever been brought forward, this is the most comprehensive and desirable, whether for navigation, drainage, or reclamation. The waters were to be carried in confined channels by the nearest route, direct into deep water; and however much the cost may have been under-rated in the above estimate, it would have been less than the amount required for the erection of the immense length of barrier banks proposed in subsequent schemes, and the value of the land reclaimed would amply compensate the original outlay.

In 1793, Captain Huddart was requested by Sir Joseph Banks to report as to whether an intended cut for bringing the Welland from its ancient course down to Spalding setway to join the Witham near Wyberton would injure the navigation to Boston, and in consequence he made a survey and report on the condition of the river at that time. Although his facts were hastily obtained from pilots and others, and the report is stated by Mr. Chapman (writing on the subject soon after), " as very erroneous and founded upon a few questions made during a few hours view of part of the channel;" yet some of his observations are very practical, and are borne out to the letter by the present state of the river. Referring to the Scalp Reach, he says, " as those flat sands accumulate and grow higher they will be subject to raise the bed of the river, which will have a bad effect upon the navigation to Boston ; for by decreasing the fall the river will be too languid to clear away the silt, and in course of time, by imperceptible degrees, the navigation will be lost to the Scalp, the channel will be subject to vary, sometimes better and at other times worse, but upon the whole it is my opinion the sands will continue to increase." Having treated on the then state of the outfall, he gives his opinion decidedly that the navigation of Boston would not be rendered worse by the intended cut for the Welland to Wyberton, at a point nearly opposite Hobhole, and he further recommended that if this were carried out that the course of the waters of the Witham should be diverted from the south to the Clayhole or North Channel; or otherwise that a cut should be made across the Scalp by the Milk-house in a right line extending from the intended junction into Clayhole, near where the present Pilot's-walk is (the preference being decidedly given to the latter plan), and that the united waters of the Witham and the Welland should be conveyed by this cut to deep water.

This is the origin of the numerous plans which have been brought forward for "*cutting through the clays,*" but with this merit belonging to it which none of its successors have, that the Welland was to be united with the Witham at a point considerably higher up than their present course, and the two rivers were to flow through the new cut ; and so the waters of the united streams would be available for keeping the channel open. The author of the scheme admits that he never saw the line of low water or took any soundings in Clayhole, but that his remarks are founded on information supplied to him.

In 1800 Mr. Rennie was directed by the Corporation "to take a survey of Boston Haven, and to report his opinion on the best mode of improving the same." He commenced his report with the following remarks :—

"The river Witham drains a very extensive tract of low and valuable land, the fall of which is so gentle, that if the seasons are in any material degree wet, it is with difficulty the water can be carried off sufficiently to enable the tenants to cultivate their lands to the best advantage. It is therefore no wonder, in so wet a season as 1799, so much of the land which drains through it should have been entirely inundated. It is true the drainage has been greatly improved in the course of these last fifty years, and Boston Haven has become considerably better ; *but it is still so crooked, and the channel so wide, that no interior works can ever make it a good outfall.* Unless, therefore, art is judiciously applied to assist nature in her operations, no material improvements must be expected to arise, at least in any moderate time."

After describing the different channels in the Deeps, and the conclusions he arrives at from his inspection of them, he proceeds :—

"It is of great importance both for the drainage and navigation, that these rivers should be carried in a proper direction to deep water, in channels sufficiently wide and deep to carry off the freshes, and to confine the tide, but not so wide as to suffer them to wander along a flat shifting beach for many miles, finding their way to deep water in numberless dribbling streams as they now do, which can neither make nor maintain a good channel."

To remedy this he proposed two plans, the one an entirely new cut; the other similar to that proposed by Captain Huddart. To quote the words of the report—the one to make a straight cut from Skirbeck Church to Clayhole of sufficient capacity for the river and navigation ; the other is to straighten and contract the present channel between Skirbeck and Hobhole, and to make thence a new cut, nearly in the direction laid down by Captain Huddart, to convey the water into Clayhole, throwing a dam across from Westmarsh Point to Hobhole Marsh. The expense of the first plan is estimated at £139,700, and the latter at £113,700. By the first plan he calculated that eight hundred and twenty acres of land would be gained by the accretion of the soil, three hundred and fifty of which were at the time salt marsh, and the remainder brown sand. By the latter plan seven hundred and sixty acres of land would be made available for reclamation, and of the estimate for this, £41,270 was for the portion between Maud Foster and Hobhole, and £72,430 for the continuation to Clayhole. Mr. Rennie concludes his report with the following remarks:—

"The improvements I have stated are confined to the channel below Skirbeck church; but when this is done, I think it will be found advantageous to make some improvements above; perhaps even to construct wet docks in some suitable situation. This, however, will be an after consideration, but ought nevertheless to be kept in view; and if some mode could be devised of establishing an accumulating fund for the purpose of repairing and improving the harbour, these different matters might be resumed as the wants of the trade should require."

In 1822 Sir John Rennie, by direction of a general meeting of all the trusts interested in the drainage and navigation, made an examination of the river, and a chart and survey, accompanied by levels and soundings, was prepared by Mr. Giles. In a very able and complete report, in which full particulars are given of the then state of the river and its outfall, the causes of the impediments to the navigation and drainage, and the remedies necessary to be applied for their removal, he recommends that the river, from the Black Sluice to Maud Foster, should be confined by jetties, and that from Maud Foster a straight cut should be made to Hobhole, adopting the old river course, where available, by training it by fascine work. This cut was to have a bottom of 80 feet at its commencement, increasing 25 feet in width for every mile, and to be excavated to a depth at Maud Foster of four feet below Hobhole cill, and increasing to five feet at Hobhole. The estimated cost was £117,190. He further recommended a continuation of this cut in the same proportion to Clayhole, and following nearly the same direction, as recommended by Captain Huddart and Mr. Rennie.

This cut was to be in a curvilinear form, bending round the corner where the present Milk-house Farm stands, the site of the present house being about the centre of the new cut, and then across the salt marshes and sands to the pilots' boat berth in Clayhole. The estimated cost of this part of the scheme was £118,467, the estimate for the complete plan being £235,658. The advantages to arise from this outlay were, that the course of the river would be shortened one third, and an increased declination of nearly twelve inches per mile thereby effected between the Black Sluice and Hobhole. In his report he views other plans which have suggested themselves, but gives this the preference as being economical and interfering less with existing works, and states that "if at any future time a dock should be required, a cut for the river could be made across to St. John's Sluice, and the old circuitous channel converted into a spacious basin of thirty acres with proper locks," &c. This would have involved the removal of the Black Sluice a quarter of a mile below Maud Foster, the cost of which would be £120,000. As to the question of the necessity of carrying out the whole of the works at once he further remarks, "The scheme, however, may with propriety terminate at Hobhole; and if found insufficient, it may be continued to Clayhole at any future period: by that time I hope that the parties connected with the river Welland, animated by a like just regard for their own interest as the parties connected with the Witham, will come forward and join them in completing this useful and important enterprise by carrying the united waters of the two rivers into Clayhole."

Unfortunately this advice was not acted upon, and consequently the improvement of the outfall has been left a legacy to the present day. In the following year Sir John Rennie was again called in, and at the same time Mr. Telford was also consulted. Mr. Telford, in a report dated March 22nd, 1823, addressed to the several trusts interested in the drainage and navigation, prefaces his remarks by saying "that the state of the haven is so apparent that it is quite superfluous to enter upon any detailed description of it." He traces the existing defects to the following causes:—First, and chiefly, to the obstruction caused by the Grand Sluice in preventing the tidal waters from flowing further up than the town of Boston. Secondly, carrying the drainage water on the fen lands on the eastern side of the river down towards Hobhole. Thirdly, suffering the river to form a crooked and wide channel by cutting away the marsh land, and becoming encumbered with mud and sand banks. To remedy the third cause he proposed a new cut from the Black Sluice across Bell's Reach to Hobhole, the expense of which he estimated at £106,846, and he states that "he proposed this scheme with the more confidence, because if the outfall even after this new channel has been made should fall into decay, still a new channel may then be extended from Hobhole to Clayhole." He concludes his report with the words, "I consider the above only a portion of the general improvement which may be executed for the drainage and navigation, but I again beg leave to repeat that I am convinced that this or any other measure must remain a temporary expedient unless the Grand Sluice is removed, and a free flux and reflux of tidal waters admitted, and I am anxious to impress upon all parties interested the imperious necessity of maintaining a perfect outfall."

Sir John Rennie's report bears the same date: he refers to his former one, and confirms the opinion therein expressed; he gives his sanction to the plan proposed by Mr. Telford, provided that Maud Foster Sluice is removed, involving a further expense beyond Mr. Telford's estimate of £18,564. He entirely concurs in Mr. Telford's remarks about the Grand Sluice, and concludes by "anxiously impressing upon all parties interested the necessity of making and maintaining a perfect outfall, without which all interior works are useless."

In 1837 a meeting of all parties interested in the drainage and navigation through the river Ouze and Lynn Deeps was held in London, and Sir John Rennie was directed to make a survey and report as to the best means of improving the same, and making it thoroughly effective. Accordingly he commenced his survey in the following year, but it was not completed till the summer of 1839. In his report he gives a short account of the various works which have been already carried out for the improvement of the Ouze, the last of these being executed from the plans and under the direction of his father, who being employed to make a general survey of the fens, ascribed the cause of the evil to the obstructed state of the Outfall of the river Ouze, which he proposed to obviate by the celebrated Eau Brink Cut, previously planned about the year 1791, and completed by him in 1818. This cut is three miles long, and shortened the course of the old river two and a half miles. Low water mark fell at Lynn as soon as the work was completed five feet, and subsequently two feet more. The reduction in the height of low water line by this work and the cut made by Kindersley, in 1773, being 10 feet 6 inches. The total cost of this and other improvements was £600,000, and the quantity of land benefitted 280,000 acres.

Sir John Rennie suggested that one general scheme for the improvement of the whole of the Estuary was far preferable to partial measures; he therefore recommended that the channels of the four rivers should be confined by fascine work, and be led to one common outlet, and that the land should be embanked as it accreted. Referring to the two rivers which are the subject of this treatise, he remarked that the Welland and Witham outfalls, particularly the former, were then in a very defective state: he suggested that they might be improved by either carrying them

x

across the clays into Clayhole, or by the Maccaroni or south channel, to join the Nene and the Ouze; the advantage of the former plan being that the distance to deep water would be considerably shorter, and in consequence it would be sooner effected; and that custom had hitherto pointed out Boston Deeps as the natural entrance or roadstead both for the Witham and the Welland. On the other hand, looking forward to one general grand plan, and the prospect of maintaining the general outfall open, he thought that there could be little doubt that the greater the body or mass of fresh and tidal water that could be brought into one channel, the better and the greater the certainty of its being able to maintain itself open. In order to effect this enlarged view of the subject, the junction of the Witham and the Welland, the Nene and the Ouze, into one common outfall, in the centre of the Great Wash, appeared the best and most certain plan; and that if the Witham and the Welland were to be carried separately into Clayhole channel, the Nene into Lynn Well, and the Ouze along the Norfolk shore, there would have been a far greater quantity of embankments to make, the channels by being separate would not have been able to maintain themselves open so well, the land gained would have been divided into several separate islands, which would have rendered it more difficult of access, and and consequently reduced its value, whilst the expense of acquiring it would have been greater; and lastly, the boundaries of the counties of Lincoln and Norfolk would have been disturbed.

The estimated quantity of land that would be gained by the union of the four rivers in one common outfall was 150,000 acres. This he estimated as being worth, in a few years, £40 per acre, or a total of £6,000,000, and after deducting £12 per acre for the expense of obtaining the greater portion, and £15 per acre for that portion lying nearest to the open ocean, would have amounted to the sum of £2,000,000, leaving a clear gain of

£4,000,000. This report was presented to a meeting held in London in July, 1839, of which Lord George Bentinck was chairman; and it was then resolved, after adopting Mr. Rennie's report, and expressing the desirability of carrying on the work, " That the execution of the same must necessarily exceed the means of private individuals, and ought therefore to receive grave consideration and the eventual support of her Majesty's Government as a purely national object." And further, that although it appeared that great improvements would be made in the various rivers and drainage of land, " The promoters of the undertaking do not feel it necessary to call either upon the landowners or the parties interested in the navigation for any contribution in the shape of tax or tonnage duty, but will rest satisfied with the reimbursements of their expenses by the acquisition of the land they expect to reclaim from the sea."

It must be a matter of the most sincere regret that this scheme, so ably planned and so warmly taken up, should have been allowed to fall to the ground. The advantages that would have accrued to the fen country would have been immense, and the increased produce obtained from the conversion of 150,000 acres of barren sands into good land, and from the improved drainage of 900,000 acres of fen country, cannot be regarded otherwise than as a national benefit. By this great undertaking not only would the navigation of the ports of Lynn, Wisbech, and Boston have been greatly improved, and the whole drainage of the fens vastly benefitted, and large sums of money saved which have since been spent on the erection of steam engines and works of interior drainage, but the whole was to be accomplished without tax or burden of any kind being imposed on the landowners.

It was not probable that so valuable a scheme should have been allowed to drop without a struggle, and twelve years afterwards it was revived in a modified and much reduced shape. A company was formed, called the "Lincolnshire Estuary Company," and an Act of Parliament obtained in 1851, "for reclaiming from the sea certain lands abutting on the coast of Lincolnshire within the parts of Holland." The capital was £600,000, to be raised by 24,000 shares of £25 each, and power was given to reclaim and embank the marsh lands adjacent to the rivers Witham, Welland, and Nene. The exact line of the new banks was: First, from a point near the sea bank at the lower end of the Nene outfall, in Long Sutton, and along the western bank of the Nene to Clayhole, and thence in a south western direction up the Welland to Fosdyke bridge. Second, commencing at the northern end of Fosdyke bridge, to continue down the Welland to the west side of Clayhole, and then curving in a western direction and continuing to the new cut end in the Witham, opposite Hobhole. Third, commencing at Hobhole sluice, and continuing in a south-easterly direction for one-and-a-half miles, and then curving in an easterly direction to the west side of Clayhole, and continuing along the channel for eight miles, and joining the old sea bank in the parish of Wrangle. The quantity to be enclosed was 30,000 acres. The owners of the marshes adjoining the lands to be vested in the company were to contribute towards the expense of making the banks, and the sum agreed on between the principal proprietors and the company was £8 15s. per acre of marsh land. The navigation and drainage of the Witham and Welland were to be improved by new cuts and outfalls, but the company was not to have any power or control in the management of the outfall.

Like its predecessor this scheme was only born to die. So many obstacles presented themselves from the scarcity of money at the time the scheme was brought out, and the difficulty of determining the rights and boundaries of the old freeholders, and the small assistance that was offered by those most to be benefitted, that the company preferred to lose all their preliminary expenses rather than proceed with the work. The time allowed by the Act for the completion of the work has now expired.

In the year 1861, Mr. Frow, of Holbeach, who has taken a great interest in the improvement of the drainage of the Fens, addressed letters to the public press, and subsequently in a communication made to the Boston Harbour Trustees, called attention to the South Channel as the proper outfall for the waters of the Witham and Welland, and he proposed that the two rivers should be trained by fascine work across the numerous beds of sands which lie at the entrance to the deeps into Lynn Well, in preference to the diversion of the waters across the scalp by the proposed cut to Clayhole, and also pointed out what he considered the defects of the latter scheme.

The season of 1860 having been unusually wet caused a great quantity of the low lands to be flooded, considerably injuring the crops throughout the Fens. The attention of the parties interested was once more aroused to the defective state of the Outfall, and the necessity of taking active steps for its improvement. The proprietors of lands in the East Fen being the greatest sufferers, the Witham Commissioners directed their engineer, the late Mr. Lewin, to make a report on the state of the whole district. Mr. Lewin's report gives some valuable statistics of facts and observations made by him of the state of the Outfall, and of the great improvement that could be effected by contracting and shortening the channel between Hobhole and deep water. He recommended the adoption of the plan laid out by Sir John Rennie for a circular cut across Hobhole Marsh to Clayhole, and in the upper part of the river the removal of the Grand Sluice, and the deepening of the bed of the Witham from Boston to Bardney.

A consideration of Mr. Lewin's report induced the Witham Commissioners to consult Mr. Hawkshaw, C.E. Under this gentleman's direction the levels of the land and principal drains in the East and West Fens were taken, and observations made as to the condition of the outfall ; and with these data to guide him, on the 29th of June, 1861, Mr. Hawkshaw made his report to the Commissioners, dividing the subject for consideration into two heads, the one comprising a plan for the improvement of the drainage of the East Fen alone, and the other, while it should effect the improvement of this district, should at the same time be more general in its application. With reference to the second plan, Mr. Hawkshaw gives it as his opinion that the project which had been recommended so frequently and for so long a period of time, viz., of forming a new cut to Clayhole, is the best as a general plan, as it would not only assist the drainage of the Fourth District, but would also improve the outfall of all the great drains which empty themselves into the Witham, and that it would benefit the navigation to and from the port of Boston. That the construction of this new channel for the Witham into Clayhole would involve the necessity of extending the Welland to a junction with it at the same point. The report further states that "In estimating the cost of the work I see no reason at present for departing from the dimensions that have been fixed by previous investigation and enquiry. They seem from such enquiry as I have been able to bestow upon them to have been judiciously determined, and they appear on former occasions to have received the sanction of the representatives of the different interests concerned. I have therefore assumed that the bottom of the cut opposite to Hobhole Sluice will be 3 feet below the cill of that sluice, and that the width of bottom at that point will be 100 feet ; the bottom to have a regular fall of one foot per mile from its commencement to its termination at Clayhole, the slopes of the sides of the cut to be four feet and a half horizontal to one perpendicular, to a height of twenty feet above the cill of

Hobhole Sluice, the foreland to be seventy feet in width. The extension of the river Welland should start at the end of the fascine work now completed, and should fall uniformly to its junction with the Witham at Clayhole. I estimate the cost of the work as under :—The Boston outfall, £80,000 ; the Welland outfall, £20,000 ; Parliamentary and engineering, say £15,000 ; —£115,000. It has been estimated by engineers who have preceded me that the extension to Clayhole would depress the low water flood level about three feet at Hobhole. It is possible that this will be the result. I am of opinion that a depression of that level to the extent of two feet can very safely be reckoned upon as a minimum at all the before-mentioned sluices. Were the depression of the flood level not to exceed that dimension it would effect a general improvement of all the districts drained through those sluices ; but as regards the navigation of Boston I am of opinion that a still greater amount of benefit would be derived, inasmuch as the low water of the river in dry weather would be depressed to a greater extent than the low water of the river in time of floods, and the channel would be scoured to an equivalent depth : while it is mainly on the depression of the low water level in the time of floods that drainage depends, the navigation will have the advantage of the former. This plan would also improve the navigation of, and the drainage into, the river Welland.

*   *   *   From all that I have read and thought on the subject it seems probable that the sands in the upper part of the estuary are steadily though slowly accumulating and encroaching on the sea. The evil effects of this can be counteracted only by training and straightening the rivers that empty themselves into the estuary, and by pushing them forward as the sea retires. The extension of the channels of the main outfall is therefore a step in the right direction, and would be a permanent step as far as it goes. Should the landowners generally not join you in the more comprehensive and general measure, I see nothing for it but to advise you to expend your money on the minor and internal scheme; but looking to the future such a step would have to be regretted. Funds that otherwise might have helped to carry out the general measure will be lost to it when the time shall arrive when all who are interested in keeping open the outfall upon which so large a tract of rich land, and so much valuable property, has been made to depend, will be driven to act vigorously to secure its existence."

At a meeting of the General Commissioners of Drainage for the river Witham, resolutions were passed adopting the principles laid down in Mr. Hawkshaw's report, and the Fourth District agreed to contribute towards a general scheme such a sum, estimated at one shilling per acre, as it would cost them to carry out the alternative scheme for the internal improvement of their own district, provided the other Trusts would at once join them in carrying out the outfall works proposed by Mr. Hawkshaw. Very strenuous efforts were made to induce all the interested parties to join in one general scheme, and a large meeting was held at the Guildhall, Boston, of representatives from the several Drainage Trusts and the Boston Harbour Commissioners; but while the necessity of an improved outfall, and the desirability of at once attempting the necessary works for ensuring it, was freely admitted, there seemed to be insuperable difficulties in reconciling the interests of the several Trusts, and the rate at which they should contribute towards the expense, and nothing was finally determined.

Foreseeing this difficulty, and relying on the very strong feeling existing at the time in favour of an improved drainage and navigation, a Bill was promoted by Mr. Thomas Wise, a gentleman who has been most indefatigable in his endeavours to bring about the improvement of the outfall, and other independent gentlemen deeply interested in the drainage and navigation, and the necessary Parliamentary notices were given for the session of 1861, but the matter was postponed till the following year, when an amended Bill was drawn up, intituled " a Bill to authorize the making of new outfalls for the rivers Witham and Welland, for improving the drainage by those rivers, and for other purposes." The object of the promoters, and the scope of the Bill, cannot be better explained than by the following quotation from a circular issued at the time :—

" The necessity for improving the drainage of the districts bordering on the rivers Witham and Welland, has been demonstrated for years past, and the evil effects of procrastination is experienced in the great and serious losses occasioned to the agriculturists on every visitation of those heavy rains which periodically fall in this locality. Throughout the country great efforts are now being made to secure practical measures for perfecting on an extensive scale an improved system of outfall drainage. With this object the Middle Level, the Nene, and the Hatfield Chase Drainage Districts are all seeking enlarged Parliamentary powers. The abundance and cheapness of capital, coupled with an increased disposition on the part of capitalists to advance large sums at a moderate rate of interest on the security of drainage rates, particularly marks the present as the proper time for making strenuous efforts to utilize the resources and capabilities of the districts and to turn to useful purposes the practical experience and suggestions of those whose valuable time has been directed to an improved measure of drainage. With this view it appears desirable to prescribe and carry out a drainage scheme adapted to the requirements of the district, with such useful modification as may be suggested, and so defined as to insure the greatest amount of benefit consistent with the least possible expense. This is proposed to be done by a Bill to be submitted to Parliament in the ensuing session, embracing powers for carrying out a plan similar to the general plan suggested by Mr. Hawkshaw, with such alterations as may be deemed expedient, and for reclaiming about 15,000 acres of marsh lands by cutting through the clays on Boston Scalp and conveying the Witham and Welland waters direct to the sea, thus shortening the distance three and a half miles, increasing the fall about six feet, and giving to the fens and uplands of Lincolnshire a most perfect and complete drainage. The entire cost of the works, including every expense, is estimated at £100,000. This charge is intended to be met by a rate or assessment upon the Commissioners and Trusts in the proportions following or as near thereto as may seem just and equitable :—The 4th District of Drainage by the river Witham, 62,276 acres, at 11½d. per acre, £3000 ; the 1st, 2nd, 3rd, 5th, and

6th Districts, 65,381 acres, at 2d. per acre, £500 ; the Welland, 34,416 acres, at 4d. per acre, £500 ; the Black Sluice, 46,215 acres, at 3d. per acre, £500 ; the Harbour of Boston on the dues of the port, £500 ;—£5000. The above charge is to remain for thirty years, when if the reclaimed land is in a condition to sell, and the Commissioners effect a sale at a price reasonably estimated at £20 per acre, the sum produced from that source would on the whole 15,000 acres be very considerable. (The Harbour Commissioners of Boston have lately sold reclaimed land of the same character after 30 years accretion at £30 per acre.) It is proposed to appropriate the sum produced as follows :—First, In repayment of the monies borrowed ; secondly, dividing the residue into three parts, two thereof to be handed over to the contributing Commissioners, and the other to be divided between the Harbour Trustees of Boston and the Trustees of the Welland. Should Parliament require provision to be made for a sinking fund, this can be done on the basis of repaying the borrowed monies in a period of thirty-five or forty years, but this would be unnecessary in the case of the reclaimed lands being realised as suggested. The Act is intended to be carried out by Commissioners to be appointed as follows :—By the Witham District, 14 ; Black Sluice, 2 ; Welland, 2 ; Boston Harbour, 2—total 20. The Fourth District Commissioners by the river Witham having called in the services of Mr. Hawkshaw, whose very able and explanatory report, with certain suggestions they have adopted, it has been considered desirable to follow up as far as practicable the recommendations therein contained, and for that purpose to ask the co-operation of the landed proprietors and others interested in the drainage, and to seek for such aid and information as may enable the parties interested to perfect a measure calculated to carry out this great and necessary work, which has never for so many years past been attempted, and the want of which annually entails such grievous losses on the district."

The promoters of this measure, after spending a considerable sum of money in preparing the necessary Parliamentary notices, and paying the other expenses incidental to obtaining an Act of Parliament, finding that they were not likely to receive that support from the landowners and others who would derive the benefit of their exertions, were obliged to withdraw their Bill, and so the outfall scheme seemed doomed to be again deferred till some greater necessity than had yet arisen should compel its adoption. After this, several of the merchants, shipowners, and traders of Boston, despairing of any improvement being ever effected in the river, and suffering from the continual lightening of the ships of their cargoes by barges, in order to enable them to reach the town, conceived the idea of carrying a railway from Boston to Freiston Shore, and there constructing a harbour where ships could lay at all times of the tide in deep water. The scheme also included the reclamation of all that valuable tract of marsh land lying adjacent to the coast at that part of the estuary. Owing to the opposition of the Drainage Trusts, and want of adequate support, the bill for the railway was withdrawn before the second reading, but the reclamation was proceeded with, and the powers therein obtained are still in existence, although no steps have yet been taken to carry out the scheme.

The dry summer of 1864, having landed up the river to such an extent that its bed was raised from ten to eleven feet at the town, and very great inconvenience and loss being experienced by those engaged in the trade of the port, at a quarterly meeting of the Harbour Commissioners held on the 27th of October, 1864, a memorial was presented by Mr Thomas Wise, "signed by the bankers, merchants, tradesmen, and shipowners of Boston, requesting that the trust would immediately take steps to improve the outfall and state of the Haven," and in accordance with the prayer of the memorial, the Commissioners resolved that Mr. Hawkshaw should be consulted and requested to frame a report upon the state of the Haven, and to recommend the best means for its improvement.

Mr. Hawkshaw made his report on the 23rd of December following, in which he states that the condition of the Haven on his examination was worse than he had before seen it. "That outside the doors of the Grand Sluice there was an accumulation of mud and sand ten to eleven feet in height above the cill. The water in the drain then standing about seven feet six inches above the cill, so that the mud outside was about three feet higher than the surface of the water inside, and that the condi-

tion of the river at the other sluices was equally bad in proportion." And this being the state of the Haven, he gives his recommendation for its improvement in the following words:—
"There are two works which, if both were executed, would effect the greatest amount of improvement in Boston Harbour, viz. First, to cut a new channel from Hobhole to Clayhole. Second, to remove the Grand Sluice and allow the tide to ebb and flow in the Upper Witham."

Mr. Hawkshaw's observations with regard to the first part of this plan have been already given. With reference to the second he remarks " The removal of the Grand Sluice would still further improve the Harbour by allowing a large quantity of water to flow into the channel, the reflux of which would increase the scouring power. This measure would require the sanction of the Commissioners for Drainage by the River Witham, and of the Great Northern Railway Company. It is not improbable that due consideration and enquiry, which would however require time, might lead these bodies to see nothing incompatible with their interests in that measure." Beyond obtaining this report no further action was at this time taken in the matter.

In the autumn of 1866, the attention of those interested in the outfall was once more aroused by the Fourth District Commissioners, despairing of any general measure being carried out, taking active steps to adopt the alternative plan recommended by Mr. Hawkshaw for the erection of pumping engines to lift the water off the lowlands in the East Fen. A strenuous effort was made to prevent, if possible, the diversion of funds to this purpose, which otherwise might be available for outfall works. There being no prospect of carrying out any of those large measures which had already been brought forward, owing to the difficulty of raising the necessary capital, a modified plan was suggested by the author of this work, in his capacity as surveyor to the

Harbour Trustees, which consisted in simply continuing the present fascine work for a distance of about two miles in the direction of Elbow Buoy, and so confining the channel in one course, the object being to direct both the flood and ebb tides in one direction, and to prevent the constant shifting of the stream amongst the sands which lie between Hobhole and the confluence of the Witham with the Welland. The effect of this training would be the more rapid discharge of the flood waters in winter; the scouring and deepening of the channel throughout its whole length; the depression of the low water mark on the cills of the several sluices; and the formation of the shifting sands into agricultural land. For the greater part of the distance the training would only be required on one side, the estimated cost of the work being £12,000.

The Harbour Trustees called in the assistance of Mr. James Abernethy, C.E., to report on the feasibility, and the advantage to be derived from the plan proposed by their surveyor, and that gentleman, in evidence subsequently given before a committee of the House of Lords, gave it his thorough sanction and support; but he also advised the dredging of the clay out of the channel between the Elbow Buoy and Clayhole, which, with some other additional works, raised the estimate to £20,000.

The experience gained from the training carried out in all the other Fen rivers, is sufficient to warrant the expectation of most favourable results from this plan, which has also the merit of the approval of those interested in the river Welland, whereas the larger scheme could not be carried out without a large expenditure of money on the part of the trustees of that river, and although calculated to effect a great improvement, owing to the increased taxation which would be rendered necessary, would meet with strenuous opposition on their part.

The present abundant supply of money in the market, and the

difficulty of finding profitable investments, appears a seasonable opportunity for reviving some of those extended schemes for reclamation of the waste land in the Estuary, and at the same time improving the outfall of the rivers. It seems an anomaly that while the country is very largely dependent on foreign supplies of corn and cattle, every possible effort should not be made to utilize every available acre of land. There are thousands of acres of land in England, which, like the marshes in this estuary, might at a less amount of money than is paid for freights of foreign grain, be turned into rich corn lands and pasture. The scheme laid out by Mr. Kindersley, and afterwards brought forward in a modified form by Sir John Rennie, for enclosing the whole of the Wash, and thus reclaiming 150,000 acres of waste space, is one worth the attention of the Government of the country. The example set by the Romans of old, who employed their soldiers, assisted by convict labour, in forming the embankments by which the Fens are protected, might well be imitated in the present day. But whether executed by public or private enterprise, there cannot be a doubt that it is high time some steps should be taken to reclaim this valuable tract of land.

www.ingramcontent.com/pod-product-compliance
Lightning Source LLC
Chambersburg PA
CBHW020827190426
43197CB00037B/721